MANAGEMENT CONTROL SYSTEMS FOR STRATEGIC CHANGES

Applying to Dematurity and Transformation of Organizations

Japanese Management and International Studies

(ISSN: 2010-4448)

Editor-in-Chief: Yasuhiro Monden *(University of Tsukuba, Japan)*

Published

For the complete list of titles in this series, please go to
http://www.worldscientific.com/series/jmis

Japanese Management and International Studies – Vol. 17

MANAGEMENT CONTROL SYSTEMS FOR STRATEGIC CHANGES

Applying to Dematurity and Transformation of Organizations

editors

Shufuku Hiraoka
Soka University, Japan

Akimichi Aoki
Senshu University, Japan

W World Scientific

NEW JERSEY · LONDON · SINGAPORE · BEIJING · SHANGHAI · HONG KONG · TAIPEI · CHENNAI · TOKYO

Published by

World Scientific Publishing Co. Pte. Ltd.

5 Toh Tuck Link, Singapore 596224

USA office: 27 Warren Street, Suite 401-402, Hackensack, NJ 07601

UK office: 57 Shelton Street, Covent Garden, London WC2H 9HE

Library of Congress Cataloging-in-Publication Data

Names: Hiraoka, Shufuku, editor. | Aoki, Akimichi, editor.

Title: Management control systems for strategic changes : applying to dematurity and
   transformation of organizations / editors, Shufuku Hiraoka, Akimichi Aoki.

Description: Hackensack : World Scientific, 2020. | Series: Japanese management and
   international studies, 2010-4448 ; vol 17 | Includes bibliographical references and index.

Identifiers: LCCN 2020021209 | ISBN 9789811219771 (hardcover) | ISBN 9789811220708 (ebook)

Subjects: LCSH: Organizational change. | Strategic planning--Management. |
   Management--Computer programs.

Classification: LCC HD58.8 .M2516 2020 | DDC 658.4/06011--dc23

LC record available at https://lccn.loc.gov/2020021209

British Library Cataloguing-in-Publication Data

A catalogue record for this book is available from the British Library.

For any available supplementary material, please visit
https://www.worldscienti ic.com/worldscibooks/10.1142/11814#t=suppl

Desk Editor: Lum Pui Yee

Typeset by Stallion Press
Email: enquiries@stallionpress.com

Printed in Singapore

Japan Society of Organization and Accounting (JSOA)

Mission of JSOA and Editorial Information

For the purpose of making a contribution to the business and academic communities, the Japan Society of Organization and Accounting (JSOA), is committed to publishing *Japanese Management and International Studies* **(JMIS), which is a refereed annual publication with a specific theme for each volume.**

The series is designed to inform the world about research outcomes of the new "Japanese-style management system" developed in Japan. However, as the series title suggests, it also promotes *"International Studies"* on the managerial competencies of various countries that include Asian countries as well as Western countries under the globalized business activities.

Research topics included in this series are management of organizations in a broad sense (including the business group or inter-firm network) and the accounting for managing the organizations. More specifically, topics include business strategy, business models, organizational restoration, corporate finance, M&A, environmental management, operations management, managerial & financial accounting, manager performance evaluation, reward systems. The research approach is interdisciplinary, which includes case studies, theoretical studies, normative studies and empirical studies, but emphasizes real world business.

Our JSOA's board of directors has established an editorial board of international standing. In each volume, guest editors who are experts on the volume's special theme serve as the volume editors. The details of JSOA is shown in its by-laws contained in the home-page: http://jsoa. sakura.ne.jp/english/index.html

Rolf G Larsson, Lund University, Sweden
Jose Antonio Dominguez Machuca, University of Sevilla, Spain
Luis E. Carretero Diaz, Universidad Complutense, Spain
Kenneth A. Merchant, University of Southern California, USA
Jimmy Y.T. Tsay, National Taiwan University, Taiwan
Stephen DunHou Tsai, National Sun Yat-Sen University, Taiwan
Yanghon Chung, KAIST, Korea
Mohammad Aghdassi, Tarbiat Modarres University, Iran
Mahfuzul Hoque, University of Dhaka, Bangladesh
Walid Zaramdini. Carthage University. Tunis.

Preface

Each organization can ensure the significance of its existence while aiming to achieve environmental sustainability. Most organizations change their strategies to match their prevailing environments. As indicated by its title, this book describes management control systems (MCS) for organizations' strategy changes. The book forms part of a series, and Volume 13 in this series, entitled *Management of Innovation Strategy in Japanese Companies*, has already discussed management control. In the present Volume 17, we provide new perspectives on this topic.

Strategy changes can include modifying the business portfolio and business model for organizational growth. Strategy changes stimulate the transformations needed for organizations to develop. The purpose of this book is to clarify how various organizations accomplish "dematurity" and transformation by utilizing technologies, changing their strategies, and ensuring proper functioning of MCS in their environments. "Dematurity" is defined herein as a broader scope not only for existing businesses but also new businesses. Our research covers various industries and organizations. The book presents many case studies of service, manufacturing, profit, and non-profit organizations. How are these organizations able to satisfy customers' and social needs? To satisfy these needs, how do they transform their products, services, business models, and organizational cultures? What are the MCSs required to evaluate these efforts? This book provides answers to these questions.

The themes of this book are:

(1) MCSs for strategy changes in an existing business portfolio (performance analysis and evaluation of business segments, synergy evaluation between segments, and asset recycling);

(2) MCSs for risk spreading between an existing core business and a diversified new business (i.e., entering a new business for the "dematurity" of an organization);

(3) MCSs for strategy changes involving digital transformation (i.e., a subscription and platform business);

(4) MCSs for strategy changes in service industries (the consistency between MCS and its approach to customers in the value co-creation process, and the impact and effect of MCSs on the productivity of the lodging industry in Japan);

(5) MCSs for strategy changes in non-profit organizations (MCS in Private Finance Initiative or Public–Private Partnership, a survey of local governments in Japan);

(6) Other topics (excessive quality in the Japanese laundry industry and the evaluation method of return on equity and strategic investment processes in semiconductor production equipment companies).

The authors of this book have conducted extensive research in fields such as strategic management accounting and MCS for service industries and non-profit organizations. In this book, we examined the relationship between strategic changes and management controls in organizations. We hope that readers will gain a deeper understanding of MCSs for strategy changes in various organizations.

We are very grateful to Ms. Lum Pui Pee, in-house editor at the World Scientific Publishing Company, for her invaluable efforts in making this volume a reality. Furthermore, we would like to express special thanks to Prof. Yasuhiro Monden of Japan Society of Organization and Accounting, who made it possible to publish this Volume 17 of the Institute.

Shufuku Hiraoka and Akimichi Aoki
August 21, 2020

About the Editors

Akimichi Aoki is Professor of Accounting, Faculty of Business Administration, Senshu University in Kanagawa, Japan, since April 2010, after he worked for Tokyo Keizai University. He is a director of the Japan Cost Accounting Association (JCAA), councilor of Japan Accounting Association (JAA), and was also an executive director of the Japanese Association of Management Accounting (JAMA) from April 2017 to March 2020. He was a Visiting Scholar of Foster School of Business at University of Washington from April 2012 to March 2013. His recent research theme is (1) revenue management in service industry (especially, lodging industry, stadium, and sharing economy) which balance short-term financial results and long-term enhancement of corporate reputation, (2) design of management control system which fits value co-creation circumstance.

Shufuku Hiraoka is Professor of Accounting, Faculty of Business Administration, Soka University, Tokyo, Japan since 2007. Prof. Hiraoka has been a president of Japan Society of Organization and Accounting (JSOA) during 2018–2019. Hiraoka was also appointed as a committee member for studying the *Practical Methods of Improvement on Productivity in Factories' Administrative Departments* of the Japan Institute of Plant Maintenance during 1993–1995. He was also a visiting scholar of the School of Management at State University of New York in Buffalo, USA, during 2007–2008. His book entitled *The Study of Financial Metrics for Corporate and Business Valuation* published in 2010 was awarded by the Business Analysis Association in Japan. His current research investigates how the business segmental reporting will be viewed from the view point of managerial Accounting.

List of Contributors

Akimichi Aoki
Professor, Faculty of Business Administration,
Senshu University, Japan

Katsuhiro Ito
Professor, Faculty of Economics,
Seikei University, Japan

Makoto Tomo
Professor, Faculty of Economics,
Seijo University, Japan

Naoya Yamaguchi
Professor, Graduate School of Professional Accountancy,
Aoyama Gakuin University, Japan

Shufuku Hiraoka
Professor, Faculty of Business Administration,
Soka University, Japan

Soichiro Higashi
Postdoctoral Researcher,
Kwansei Gakuin University, Japan

Takehiro Metoki
Associate Professor, Graduate School of Accountancy,
Waseda University, Japan

Tohru Furuyama
Associate Professor, Faculty of Management and Economics,
Kaetsu University, Japan

Tsutomu Yoshioka
Associate Professor, Faculty of International Tourism Management,
Toyo University, Japan

Yasuhiro Monden
Professor Emeritus,
Tsukuba University, Japan

Zhi Wang
Associate Professor, Faculty of Economics,
Sophia University, Japan

Contents

Part 1

Management Controls for Business Changes

Chapter 1

Risk Spreading between the Diversified Subscription Businesses and the Existing Business: Focusing on the Case of Apple

Yasuhiro Monden

Professor Emeritus of Tsukuba University,
Tsukuba, Ibaraki 305-8577, Japan

Prologue

(1) **Teachings of "Risk Sharing"** to reduce the risk for a pair of individuals.

> *Two are better than one, because they have a good return for their labor:*
> *If either of them falls down, one can help the other one up. But pity*
> *anyone who falls and has no one to help them up.*

The Old Testament, Ecclesiastes, 4: 9–12

The readers should note that this saying starts with the word "Two," which means "two people" or "two companies," which could be a wife and her husband, teacher and student, or a holding company and its subsidiary. Both the people and the companies in this pair are independent but cooperate with each other. Consider the case of independent but allied companies. When a subsidiary company is facing bankruptcy, the paternal company may help it. Think of the relationship between an automobile company and its allied parts supplier (often called *a detail-controlled parts supplier*). When the supplier is unable to cover its fixed costs for manufacturing the parts to be supplied to the automaker, the automobile maker will help to compensate the fixed cost of the parts. This is known as a *risk sharing* relationship (See Monden and Nagao (1988)).

(2) **Teachings of "Risk Spreading"** to reduce the risk for investors in multiple projects.

> *Ship your grain across the sea; after many days you may receive a return. Invest in seven ventures, yes, in eight; you do not know what disaster may come upon the land.*

The Old Testament, Ecclesiastes 11

Readers should note that this saying starts with the phrase "your grain." Thus, it assumes "only one person or one company" at the beginning. It is only an individual who scatters seeds in several fields or only one company that invests its funds in several venture companies (or "start-up" firms). Then, in the case of a disaster, it may not be possible to obtain good results from all the fields or all firms you have invested in, but it is more likely that you will see good results when there is a higher possibility of *risk spreading* among various opportunities.

Consider a Japanese *mega-supplier* that manufactures electronics parts for the automobile industry. Because this mega-supplier (often called a *black-box parts maker*) is technically excellent, it can supply parts to several automakers. Thus, even if this mega-supplier is unable to supply products to a certain automaker, it will be able to provide products to other automakers. Therefore, the company continues to make higher profits, thanks to its *risk spreading* ability on account of its high technical capability (See Monden and Nagao (1988)).

(3) **"Life Cycle"** of any person or merchandise.

> *The sound of Gion Shoja bells echoes the impermanence of all things; the color of Sala flowers reveals the truth that the prosperous must decline. The proud do not endure; they are like a dream on a spring night.* (*Gion Shoja* is the name of the temple built for the Buddha.)
> Heike Monogatari (*The Tale of the Heike*) (mid-13th century)

McCullough (1988)

This proverb means everything has its own life cycle, including manufacturing products whose stages of life are infancy, growth, maturity, and finally, decline, but this cycle can be reversed through industrial "dematurity." In the case of the life cycle of industrial products, any product may eventually decline. For example, even sales of Apple's smartphone (iPhone) seem to have declined recently. To solve the problem of this decline, Apple is going to apply the concept of "risk spreading" between their smartphone business and other service businesses. Thus, we will examine how they cope with this situation via "subscription" service businesses.

1. Research Theme

1.1 *"Risk spreading" in the business portfolio*

This study first investigates the reason for the recent emergence of the "subscription" business model in the field of digital business as conducted by Google, Apple, Facebook, and Amazon (GAFA) and then theoretically examines the "risk spreading" in a company that has subscription businesses from the viewpoint of the *business portfolio* strategy. The study then analyzes various forms of actual subscription businesses.

In addition, from the "security" *portfolio* selection as well as "business" *portfolio* decision theories, the current study clarifies whether the subscription business in the digital field can contribute to the goal of "risk spreading."

Finally, the study examines the recent case of the subscription businesses launched by Apple and clarifies whether their business model can satisfy the risk spreading goal.

1.2 *Why has the subscription business emerged?*

1.2.1 *What are the reasons for the emergence of the subscription business?*

One of the main reasons the subscription business has recently become popular is because the sales of hardware products have recently decreased, creating a need to compensate for this reduction in *hardware* sales by increasing *service* sales.

This idea could also be rephrased as follows: From the *high-risk and high-return* business model of selling physical products to the *low-risk and low-return* business model of selling a service.

This change in the business models can further be likened to a transition from *buying and selling* to *lease or rent* in real estate businesses. *Capital gains* from selling a condominium could result from the former, while *income gain* from renting the condominium to a person could result from the latter.

The subscription business in this study resembles the latter business, which is low risk and low return, while the manufacturing and selling of the physical products resemble the buying/selling aspect of real estate businesses, which entails high risk and high return. However, it is not possible to determine which business model is better. It depends on personal characteristics or attitudes toward the risk. That is, it depends on whether the investor is *risk seeking* (preferring a high-risk and high-return business) or *risk averse* (preferring low-risk and low-return businesses).

Among these two types of businesses, the flat-rate subscription business belongs to the low-risk, low-return type, which enables the *smoothing of the sales revenue* or smoothing of the monthly profits.

2. Two Types of Subscription Businesses: Flat-Rate System and the Usage-proportional Rate System

The flat-rate system is a contract that enables users to watch movies or listen to music as many times as they want once they have paid a monthly flat-rate fee. Under this system, once users have paid the monthly fixed amount of the fee, the amount will not be refunded even if they do not use the service at all. However, even if a subscriber uses the service multiple times, the fee does not change. Thus, for such users, the fee for one-time usage of service will decrease. As a result, this system may increase customer loyalty so that the company is able to increase the number of successive users.

The usage-proportional rate system is often applied to *sharing services* such as "car sharing," "lodging," and so on, which use the usage-proportional rate system and charge only for the number of times or hours the service is used. This system is popular because the user does not need to pay any fees if they do not use the service. Such a system will be convenient for those who will not use a particular service frequently, such as luxury car rental. (For details of the two types of subscriptions, see Tzuo and Weisert (2018).)

3. "Risk Spreading" Through the Business Diversification from the Viewpoint of the Portfolio Selection Theory

3.1 *Maturation of the life cycle of the main businesses in Google, Apple, Facebook, and Amazon*

The return on sales (or net profit on sales) of large internet-related companies such as GAFA has fallen from 26% in 2012 to less than 20% in 2019 (*The Nikkei*, 2019.02.26). The main reason for such a slowdown is due to a decrease in sales growth of their main businesses, such as the decline of iPhone sales. This means that GAFA's main businesses have recently declined.

3.2 *Diversification strategy to cope with the maturity in the business life cycle*

3.2.1 *What is the diversification strategy as risk spreading? Analysis from the viewpoint of the portfolio selection in security investment*

The portfolio selection theory of various security investments was first proposed by Markowitz (1952), and this study applies his theory to the portfolio problem of diversified businesses.[1]

---

[1] The portfolio in the security investment is a set of various stocks that will be held by an investor. The decision to have such a set of securities is called the optimal portfolio selection. The basic decision rule for formulating such a portfolio is as follows:

(a) The investor not only wishes to maximize the *expected revenue* from their stock investment but also attempts to minimize the risk from their investment. Such risk could be measured by the *variance* surrounding the expected value of their revenue.
(b) Various investment opportunities (i.e., revenues from various securities) are not mutually independent. That is, various investment opportunities will move in the same or

Suppose that the price of stock A is highly *correlated* with the price of stock B. That is, if the price of A goes up, the price of B will also increase, and vice versa. Also, if the price of A goes down, the price of B will also decrease, and vice versa. In such a case, the risk of the total portfolio of two such securities will increase; such an investment in two brands will be *high risk and high return*.

On the contrary, if the correlation of prices between two different stocks is lower, then the investment in such stocks will be *low risk and low return*. Due to their *risk-aversive* behavior or *risk spreading* investment, such a security investment portfolio will be created if the investor favors *low risk and low return*.

3.2.2 *"Risk spreading" through the business diversification strategy from the viewpoint of portfolio theory: Case of Apple*

Since selling smartphones as hardware merchandise has declined, Apple has decided to extensively move into new *"service* businesses" such as the movie, music, and game-selling services. Thus, it seems that Apple

---

in the opposite direction with the revenue of the entire security market or with the revenue of the other securities. Such mutual relationships between various securities could be statistically measured by the *co-variance* or by the *correlation coefficient.*

Under the above general relationship, the security investor will make his or her decision about the trade-off (or priority) between the *expected revenue* (i.e., average revenue to be gained) and the *variance* (i.e., various values of revenues).

In such a situation, when the value of the portfolio of the security market as a whole (i.e., the general index of stock price such as "Nikkei average," "TOPICS," or Dow–Jones stock average) will significantly increase, the stock price of a certain company may also increase at the same time (i.e., positive correlation) or it may decrease inversely (i.e., negative correlation). For example, *the stock prices of the companies that are producing the complementary goods may show correlated behavior.* If such complementary stocks are held, then a "high return" may be obtained if you are lucky, but you may incur a big loss if you are unlucky. However, if the stocks of *rival* firms in the same industry are held, then stock prices of such firms may show negative correlation (or adverse correlation). That is, loss may be smaller even if you are unlucky, or a low return may be obtained even if you are lucky.

regarded such an expansion of business brands as a kind of "risk spreading" strategy between iPhone and the new service businesses.

Unlike Apple's intention, however, *their diversification strategy could not be regarded as a risk spreading strategy.* The reason is that Apple is attempting to use iPhone sales, which has been their most profitable business, to increase business in other areas. Apple has attempted to increase the sales of their new service businesses under the assumption that *their customers will make good use of iPhones* to enjoy movie and games services, and so on (i.e., subscription business).

However, *declining* iPhone sales do not correlate with the increased sales of their new subscription services. In other words, *since iPhones sales are weak, their sales of new services would also be weak,* and their diversification businesses would therefore form a "high-risk" pattern as a portfolio. Let us check how the real situation is in Apple.

3.2.3 *Shorter length of usage time for iPhone is under competition among various "contents" attractiveness*

As of December 2018, the average number of hours of smartphone use per day is 3 hours and 5 minutes in Japan. In addition, since services such as music, movie, games, and news can all be accessed via a smartphone, there is likely to be fierce competition among various services at certain times.

Therefore, because there is competition among various services for the "limited timespan of usable time" for smartphones, it will not be possible for Apple to meet the expectations of these services. That is, decreasing iPhone sales would not be compensated by increasing sales of new service businesses; therefore, adverse or negative correlation between two businesses would *not* be possible.

However, if adverse correlation occurred between the aforementioned two businesses, then it follows that the *variance* of profitability of the portfolio of *both* businesses will be statistically smaller than that of *each* business. The risk of the portfolio will therefore be smaller and the effect of risk spreading could be gained.

3.2.3.1 Risk figure β_i of each business i in a diversified company

Monden and Fernand (1995) developed a mathematical model to derive the *risk figure* of each business in the diversified company, using the measure of *the sensitivity of how the change of profitability of a certain business will vary depending on the changes of total profitability of the whole portfolio of the businesses of the company a whole.* This risk figure is β_i for each business in a company, which is similar to the β_i of the capital asset pricing model (CAPM).[2]

3.2.3.2 Three-dimensional "Product Portfolio Management"

Suppose that there are many hundreds of divisions or subsidiary firms in a large diversified company, and each subsidiary firm conducts each business of the diversified parent company. Then, by applying the risk coefficient β_i of each business, the top management of the diversified parent company can use the following three measures for each business: (1) growth rate of sales, (2) rate of profitability, and (3) risk rate. The growth and profitability were proposed by the Boston Consulting Group matrix (BCG matrix), while the risk measure β_i of each business i was also added

---

[2]Markowitz (1952) pioneered the theory of portfolio selection for stock investment, and Monden (2001) introduced the quadratic programming model of optimal portfolio selection. Further, Sharp (1964), Lintner (1965), and Mossin (1973) were the pioneers of CAPM.

In addition, Monden and Fernand (1995) proposed a new model to show the "risk" measure of each business in the multi-brand (diversified) company. The essence of our diversified company model is as follows:

Denote:

$$\beta_i = \mathrm{cov}_{i\rho} / (\sigma_\rho)^2$$
$$= r_{i\rho}\sigma_i\sigma_\rho / (\sigma_\rho)^2$$

where $\mathrm{cov}_{i\rho}$ is the covariance of business Xi and business $X\rho$, $r_{i\rho}$ is the correlation coefficient between the revenue rate of business i and the revenue rate of the business portfolio, σ_i is the standard deviation of the revenue of the business Xi, σ_ρ is the standard deviation of the revenue of the business portfolio β.

Here the value of β_i is how the revenue of business i will move in response to the change of the revenue of the business portfolio as a whole.

by Monden and Fernand (1995), and the authors refer to this model as a *three-dimensional model of Product Portfolio Management*.[3]

4. The Manufacturing Company to be Transformed to a Service Company: Case Study of Apple's Subscription Business

4.1 *Three categories of Apple's businesses*

Apple began to introduce flat-rate services to recover the decrease in smartphone sales. We first examine their current financial performance (see Table 1).

Table 1. Quarterly sales of each business segment of Apple (million dollars).

	Three months ended		
Net sales by each business	Dec. 29, 2018	Dec. 30, 2017	Change rate
iphone	$51,982	$61,104	(15)%
Mac	7,416	6,824	9%
ipad	6,729	5,755	17%
Wearables, Home and Accessories	7,308	5,481	33%
Services	10,875	9,129	19%
Total of net sales	$84,310	88,294	(5)%

---

[3] According to the BCG matrix, each business is classified into one of the four categories: *Star, Cash-cow, Dog, and Question-mark*. Since we have added the risk measure into the above four categories, each of these categories will be additionally evaluated by considering whether they are "risky" or "safer" depending on if β_i is < or ≥1, or equal to 1, or minus. Thus, the classifications will be [*prospective Goose* or *risky Goose*], [*prospective Star* or *risky Star*], [*pet Dog* or *biting Dog*], or [*prospective Child* or *questionable Child*], and so on.

However, it should be noted that the measure of β_i implies whether or not the business in question will be influenced by the average profitability of the whole portfolio of businesses. Thus, if β_i is bigger than 1, then business i will be regarded as being safer compared to the move of the business of the company as a whole.

There are many other studies of the mathematical models for the *diversified business portfolio strategy*. Examples are Bettis and Mahajan (1980), Rabino and Wright (1984), Carzo and Wind (1985), and Colin and Ruefli (1992), among others.

4.1.1 *Apple's existing hardware merchandise*

Hardware products sold by Apple include the iPhone, iPad, iPod, Mac, Apple Watch, and so on. As shown in the quarterly statement of Apple's segmented sales from October to December 2018, iPhone sales have decreased compared to the same quarter in 2017.

Total corporate sales of the company as a whole decreased by 5% to 84,310 million dollars. The reasons are as follows: iPhone sales decreased 15% to 51,982 million dollars to the same quarter of last year 2017, and as a result, the sales ratio of iPhones to total corporate sales also decreased from 69.2% to 62%. This was the reduction just after 9 years.

However, the sales of the services of the quarter ended in Dec. 29, 2018 has considerably increased by 19%, compared to the sale of the same quarter ended in Dec. 30, 2017 (See Table 1). When we notice this point Apple's busines model is enjoying the "risk spreading" between the declining iPhone business and the increasing Services business.

4.1.2 *The new subscription businesses*

From September 2019, Apple decided to introduce four flat-rate subscription services, as shown in the right-hand side of Fig. 1.

4.2 *New subscription strategy*

4.2.1 *Apple TV + and Apple Arcade*

Apple TV + is a flat-rate movie service and Apple Arcade is a flat-rate *game service.*[4] Both have been introduced to rebuild the company as a whole after its decline.

---

[4] *Apple's game and the Cloud Streaming Game*
Apple's new game service based on the flat-rate system is to be a so-called Cloud Streaming Game, which uses massive volumes of cloud data. A cloud game uses the game software of the massive volume of data in the "cloud," which is a large internet-based data center. From such a cloud, the game data are *sequentially* received and reproduced as a game on a smartphone or iPad. This game service is based on the technique known as *streaming*.

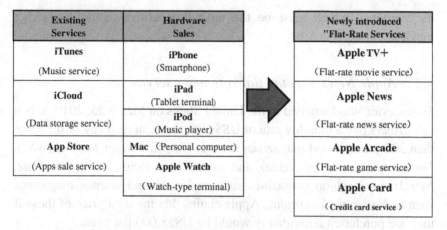

Existing Services	Hardware Sales	Newly introduced "Flat-Rate Services
iTunes (Music service)	iPhone (Smartphone)	Apple TV+ （Flat-rate movie service）
iCloud (Data storage service)	iPad (Tablet terminal) iPod (Music player)	Apple News （Flat-rate news service）
App Store (Apps sale service)	Mac （Personal computer） Apple Watch （Watch-type terminal）	Apple Arcade （Flat-rate game service） Apple Card （Credit card service ）

Fig. 1. Existing services, hardware sales, and new flat-rate businesses.

Source: Adapted from *The Nikkei* (2019.03.27a, 2019.03.27b, 2019.03.27c).

There are many rival companies in the movie and game services business competing throughout the world.

Since 60% of young people aged 18–29 use flat-rate movie services instead of the toll TV movie, Apple is also facing a challenge selling their movies to this age group.

4.2.1.1 The characteristics of Apple's movie services based on the iPhone business

Apple has attempted to utilize the iPhone platform since it is still earning huge revenue from this at present. However, the smartphone is now under *commoditization* due to the growth of Chinese and Korean companies and Apple may not continue their high-end marketing policy as before.

Under the "5G" technology of the next generation of global communication, younger people will be able to watch movies via smartphones. The critical factors may be how Apple sets the price of movie services and

---

For example, Sony has been using the "PlayStation" games console for a long time, but they recently began using the "PlayStation Now" for cloud streaming games. Microsoft recently began to affiliate with Sony, and they are co-developing a cloud service game system.

its "content," which must be the most competitive factor in internet movies.

4.2.2 *Apple News + as the flat-rate news service*

This service was launched in the United States on March 25, 2019. When subscribers pay a monthly rate of US$9.99, they can read any of the more than 300 journals and magazines such as *The Wall Street Journal* (*WSJ*), *Fortune* (economic magazine), and so on. Other examples include *Time*, *New Yorker*, fashion magazines such as *Vogue*, and science magazines such as *National Geographic*. Apple claims that the total price of these if they are purchased individually would be US$8,000 per year.

4.2.2.1 Competition between "Apple News +" and individual journals

The Wall Street Journal (*WSJ*) sells its own *online journal* at their own flat rate of $40 per month.

Because WSJ's online journal is in competition with "Apple News + ," *WSJ* online service may not be able to compete with Apple News + as a whole. From such a viewpoint, some of the large online journals do not participate in Apple News + .

WSJ, however, may have decided to participate in Apple News + because they may be able to obtain additional readers if they participate in Apple's *ecosystem*[5] because there are 14 billion iPhone users.

4.2.2.2 Competition for revenue allocation between "Apple News +" and the collected individual journals

"Apple News +" may compete with the participating journals and magazines for the allocation of their revenues. Apple demands 50% of the total revenue, but it is reported that the participating content providers such as *WSJ*, *Time*, and *Vogue* are accusing Apple of being greedy (*The Nikkei*, 2019.03.27a, 2019.03.27b, 2019.03.27c).

---

[5] Refer to Monden (2014) and Monden (2018, Chapter 9, pp. 213–214), for details of Apple's "ecosystem."

Suppose that Apple computes the gross margin from the market sales of "Apple News +" by applying the following formula:

Gross margin = total revenue from subscription fees
$\qquad$ − full costs of Apple News +.

However, there must be additional *opportunity costs* on the side of WSJ, for example. This is the amount of reduced sales due to the decrease in the number of readers caused by the market sales of "Apple News +." Thus, WSJ will demand at least as much *additional profit* as will be lost due to participation in Apple News + .

We now calculate how the royalties from all the movies, music, electronic journals, content, and so on will be allocated to the content provider firms.

In the case of flat-rate internet services, the allocation rate of the total royalties will be determined by the following formula, depending on (1), (2), (3), and so on (*The Nikkei*, 2019.05.23):

(1) Number of content providers
(2) Number of subscribers
(3) Total amount of advertisement revenues

Allocated amount of total royalties for content provider j

$\geq$ [(flat-rate subscription fee) × (total number of subscribers) + advertising revenue − full cost paid by platformer]

× ([(list price Pj of the journal j) × (sales quantity Mj of journal j in the internet group service)]

$/\Sigma$ $(Pj \times Mj)$}, where $j = 1, 2, ..., n$ (n = total number of the included journals).

In the above formula, the right-hand side of the equation indicates the *opportunity cost* paid by the participating content provider j. According to the *cooperative game theory*, if the opportunity cost of participant j is at least compensated by the transformer (i.e., the cooperative group leader), there will be no complaint among the participants regarding the cooperation (see Monden, 2018).

5. Conclusion: The Relationship between the iPhone Business and the New Service Businesses

This section summarizes whether Apple's new subscription business could achieve the *risk spreading* effect in their entire business portfolio.

The new flat-rate service business (business B) was introduced for the purpose of recovering the decline of iPhone sales (business A) (See Table 1). Thus, it is assumed that *risk spreading* between these two kinds of businesses could be achieved.

For A and B to achieve reducing the whole risk as a whole of the company, there must be an *adverse correlation* between business A (i.e., iPhone) and business B (i.e., new subscription businesses). That is, even though the revenue from iPhones may decrease continuously, the revenue of the new business B must *increase*, so that the risk of the company as a whole must be at least minimized. Apple has succeeded in their business of iPhone developed by Mr. Steve Jobs, one of co-founders. That was the typical technical innovation. Meanwhile, the sales of their high-grade iPhone has decreased in China due to their own low-end smartphone since 2018.

Thus Mr. Tim Cook, the present CEO, has introduced the new service business, "subscription business," since 2019, which has been discussed in this paper. They have succeeded in this new business, covering the decline of iPhone, and have increased the total sales and total profit of the company. (The sales in the first quarter of 2020 was increased by 17% compared to the last year, which was 13,348 million dollars, the highest quarterly sales of the company.)

Following this success of new service business, Mr. Tim Cook has proudly said to the security analysts (in 2020. 05.25) that **"we have always overcome the hard situation by investing in the next generation technical innovation"** However, accurately speaking this service business was not a "technological" innovation, but the "subscription business" which has been adopted by many companies such as video streaming service by Netflix, etc.

However, since any business will have a lifecycle as like as any creature, the market of this new service business will also encounter the maturity stage and get into the decline stage. Then what business will Apple get into? For example, could Apple again make any technical innovation as Steve Jobs has developed iPhone?

In the world of biological creatures only the one who could have adapted the environmental change can survive. Even though their change is just a change at random, as a reverse of *"mutant,"* they could succeed in the "evolution" as a *"survival for fittest."* The author would like to hope that that Apple also would make such an endless evolution from now on, too.

References

Bettis, R.A. and Mahajan, V. (1980). Risk/return performance of diversified firms, *Management Science*, Vol. 31, No. 7, pp. 785–799.

Carzo, R.N. and Wind, K. (1985). Risk return approach to product portfolio strategy, *Long Range Planning*, Vol. 18, No. 2, pp. 77–85.

Colin, J.M. and Ruefli, T.W. (1992). Strategic risk: An ordinal approach, *Management Science*, Vol. 38, No. 12, pp. 1707–1731.

Lintner, J. (1965). The valuation of risk assets and the selection of risky investment in stock portfolios and capital budgets, *The Review of Economics and Statistics*, Vol. 47, No. 1, pp. 13–37.

Markowitz, H.M. (1952). Portfolio selection, *Journal of Finance*, Vol. 7, No. 1, pp. 77–91.

Monden, Y. and Nagao, T. (1988). Full cost-based transfer pricing in the Japanese auto industry: Risk-sharing and risk-spreading behavior. *Journal of Business Administration*, Vol. 17, Nos. (1–2), pp. 117–136. Revised and reprinted in Monden, Y. (ed.), (2018), Chapter 18.

Monden, Y. (ed.) (2001). Basis of portfolio selection: Average and variance model, *Managerial Accounting: Strategic Finance and Decentralized Management*, Chapter 14. Tokyo: Zeimu Keiri Kyokai (in Japanese).

Monden, Y. and Fernand, W.F.H. (1995). Business portfolio strategy under risk, *JICPA Journal*, Vol. 7, No. 5, pp. 20–30 (in Japanese).

Monden, Y. (2014). Lean management of global supply chain: Optimal combination of market, product design, supply chain, and lifecycle, in Monden, Y. and

Minagawa, Y. (eds.), *Lean Management of Global Supply Chain*, Chapter 1. Singapore: World Scientific Publishing Co. Pte. Ltd.

Monden, Y. (2018). *Economics of Incentives for Inter-Firm Network*. Singapore: World Scientific Publishing Co. Pte. Ltd.

Mossin, J. (1973). *Theory of Financial Markets*. Englewood Cliffs NJ.: Prentice-Hall.

Rabino, S. and Wright, A. (1984). Applying financial portfolio and multiple criterion approaches to product line decisions, *Industrial Marketing Management*, Vol. 13, pp. 233–240.

Sharp, W.F. (1964). Capital asset prices: A Theory of market equilibrium under condition of risk, *Journal of Finance*, Vol. 19, No. 3, pp. 425–442.

Tzuo, T. and Weisert, G. (2018). *Subscribed: Why the Subscription Model will be Your Company's Future — and What To Do About It*. New York: Portfolio/Penguin.

Further Readings (all in Japanese)

The Nikkei (2019.02.06). GAFA earning power was reduced: Change of high growth and the social cost became heavy due to their customer data management and social restriction.

The Nikkei (2019.03.27a). Apple will enter the movie service: Flat-rate services will begin in autumn 2019.

The Nikkei (2019.03.27b). Apple will participate in flat rate movies but protect customer data.

The Nikkei (2019.03.27c). Apple will deliver the new flat rate service: Struggle for the revenue allocation.

The Nikkei (2019.05.17). Cloud games are popular by smartphone.

The Nikkei (2019.05.23). Revenues must be allocated to the content makers in Apple's new services.

The Nikkei (2019.06.05). Apple enters the flat rate subscription services in movie, music, and games.

Chapter 2

Management Control Concepts to Foster Organizational Ambidexterity

Katsuhiro Ito

Faculty of Economics, Seikei University,
Tokyo 180-8633, Japan

1. Problem Setting

The last three decades of sluggish growth of various economic indicators and the declining global presence of Japanese companies has been described as *the lost 30 years*. Specific factors behind this economic stagnation include: (1) Japan's failure to shift to a system of globally horizontal division of labor, as created through the industrialization of emerging countries, including China, and (2) Japan's inability to produce a global platformer due to delayed responses to digitalization. Several problems require resolution. Undeniably, Japan has failed to adapt smoothly to changing environments. With shortening business lifecycles, the efficient management of existing businesses alone does not enable adaptation to future environment changes. Considering this, there has long been emphasis on the dematurity strategy, a business challenge against the end of existing business. This challenge is difficult to solve but deserves serious consideration.

This dematurity strategy has been discussed for some time. Since the 1990s, it has been formulated as the innovator's dilemma and has gained attention. According to Christensen (1997), a new business or technology is not sufficiently lucrative for a company with a strong market presence to invest in and even causes a conflict of interest with the existing business, through cannibalization. It has been noted that companies tend to focus too much on deepening their existing business ("continuous innovation," which improves predecessors) and therefore, are inevitably late in entering a new technical field ("disruptive innovation," which destroys predecessors). Excellent corporations listen to their clients, increase production according to their preference, and actively invest in new technologies for improvement. Although it is necessary and desirable to optimize the company for the existing business, it precludes responses to disruptive innovation that could significantly change the market structure. The harder a company works, the deeper it falls. This is a frightening situation.[1]

In these lost 30 years, start-ups born in the Silicon Valley have become a global trend. The energy applied in establishing these start-ups is now spreading from advanced countries to emerging countries. Looking back, the failure to build an ecosystem to create new businesses[2] and absorb the energy of such start-ups seems to be major factors behind the failure to adapt to changes in the environment during these 30 years.

New business creation and business structure transformation against the maturation of existing businesses have become inevitable for a company to survive. This chapter discusses how management control should contribute to the dematurity strategy.

---

[1] This problem resembles a case of "productivity dilemma" as discussed by Abernathy (1978). Abernathy (1978) pointed out that innovation is largely divided into product innovation and process innovation, which stand in a trade-off relationship with each other.

[2] Ecosystem (business ecosystem) refers to the relationship among companies and businesses as likened to a natural ecosystem. This concept has been growing in importance, since a single business or company alone does not perform business operations. In its original meaning, an ecosystem contains producers, consumers, and decomposers. The energy absorbed by a producer (plant in this case) through photosynthesis is used by a consumer (animal) through a food chain. The corpses and excretions of producers and consumers are decomposed into inorganic compounds mainly by decomposers (microorganisms, etc.). A complex interdependent relationship forms an entire physical cycle in nature. A company cannot survive if it fails to build a relationship with others, and does everything alone.

2. Changing Environment of Evolutionary Adaptedness (EEA) Surrounding Management Control

2.1 *Formulation and development of the management accounting theory in the U.S.*

Management control does not easily contribute to the dematurity strategy. In the context and the times in which the concept of management control was formulated, there was little emphasis on the issue of new business creation. Therefore, an approach different from the conventional framework is required. It is necessary to understand that the environment of evolutionary adaptedness (EEA) surrounding the existing theory has been changing.

What is the EEA? It refers to a collection of efficient causes affecting the environmental adaptation process of organisms. When one individual with a given attribute gains an advantage in surviving and reproducing over another individual with no such attribute, that psychological mechanism should spread across the whole species through the process of natural selection. On the contrary, it could be presumed that when a given attribute is recognized universally in many individuals of the same species, it must have played certain roles beneficial to successful survival and reproduction in the history of that species' evolution.

The management accounting theory, a core of management control, was developed to respond to the expanding scale of management and the increasingly complex internal production processes in the late 19th century and beyond. The theory was then established in the 1920s, based on the ideas of "setting standards" and "comparing actual performance with the set standards" (Hiromoto, 1993). Standard cost accounting and budget management were the major calculation methods in the formative period of management accounting theory. These standard-oriented thoughts are intended to remove dispersion and variation. Management accounting theory evolved mainly in the U.S., where large corporations were concentrated. Hiromoto (1993) classified the history of this theory into the following four periods: formation (1919–1929), growth (1930–1945), establishment (1946–1966), and evolution (1966 and beyond). As management issues increased with the increasing size and complexity of organizations, various techniques were developed to refine a theoretical system. Despite vigorous discussions on the management of research and development activities, there has been much less focus on the process of creating new businesses than on the efficient execution of existing businesses. The primary mission of conventional management accounting was to smoothly implement business strategies of bigger and increasingly complex organizations. As business life shortens, the emerging challenge is to create a new business, besides operating the existing business. New business creation requires various trials and errors, rather than reducing variation. The EEA that was beneficial for corporations that effectively use conventional management accounting might have now changed greatly.

2.2 *History of the management control theory*

The role of management control is to encourage organization members to adopt desired behaviors. Authentic, full-scale research on the management control theory was led by Anthony (1965), who categorized a business management system into strategic planning, management control, and operational control. In the 1960s, the core of management control was management accounting information (management control almost equaled management accounting). Management control was expected to ensure the efficient implementation of the existing strategy within the framework of a strategic plan.

Since the 1980s, the role expected of management control has come to include both implementing and exploring a management strategy (see Fig. 1). This is partly because of the blurring of boundaries between

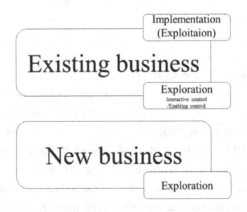

Fig. 1.　Development of the management control theory.

strategic planning and management control, making it harder to ignore the currents in both directions (*interactive control* was conceptualized). It is also because operational control needs to be improved, which requires the incorporation of management control elements (in the form of *enabling control*). When both implementation and exploration are required, management accounting is not the only major player of management control (control tools), and there were active discussions on a control package, including control by management philosophy and organizational culture. The relation between management control and management accounting has changed from approximately equal to management control gaining an upper hand on management accounting.

In pursuing exploration, new methods of using management accounting information have been theorized. However, the exploration of both interactive control and enabling control was with an emphasis on the existing business. To create a new business, proper exploration, away from the existing business and within a long range, is expected from management control.

Furthermore, based on the concept of business ecosystem, management control does not necessarily target the company's internal community alone. Suppliers and customers in and beyond company boundaries are now included in management control.

The history of the management control theory from 1965 is as follows:

1. Management control has expanded in scope, including both implementation and exploration (strategic planning and business process are no longer exogenous variables of management control).
2. Management control has been recognized as a collection of various control tools (control package).
3. Management control also targets other companies outside a given business boundary (emphasis on business ecosystem).

To solve the "dematurity strategy issue," it is necessary to motivate organization members to create a new business through trial and error in a situation where the right answer is not apparent in advance. The characteristics mentioned above will become more noticeable in that process.

3. Balancing Exploration and Implementation

3.1 *Organizational ambidexterity*

"Organizational ambidexterity" is the skillful achievement of smoothly operating the existing business and exploring a new business simultaneously (O'Reilly and Tushman, 2013, 2016).

Most people have one dominant arm, while very few have two dominant arms. In this case, ambidexterity refers to the simultaneous pursuit and achievement of exploration to expand one's scope of knowledge through trials and errors in unknown fields and exploitation[3] ($\approx$ implementation, exploitation, deepening) to use the existing knowledge in real settings and increase accuracy. Implementing and exploiting are used interchangeably in this chapter without making a precise distinction.

An important aspect of organization ambidexterity is to attain a proper balance between exploration through trials and errors for the future and exploitation (deepening) to secure current achievements.

March (1991) first identified these two lines of thought — exploration and exploitation — and approached an organizational learning process from these viewpoints. Exploration is the activity to gain new insights separate from the existing knowledge, while exploitation is organizational learning activity to deepen existing knowledge. These are two different activities of organizational learning. He noted that a key issue is the distribution of resources to each.

March (1991) argued that an appropriate combination of both is necessary for sustainable organization development, rather than relying heavily on either exploration or exploitation. Exploitation alone does not enable proper response to changing environments due to lack of diversity, although it may maximize short-term performance. Still, neglecting exploitation and rigid preoccupation with exploration will not allow companies to recover the resources necessary for survival.

---

[3]Whether an existing scope of defense is expanded determines the classification of exploration or exploitation. The latter implies the use of existing knowledge, execution of fixed operations, or deepening of existing knowledge. Therefore, Japanese translation is used appropriately, depending on context; however, all of them indicate exploitation (against exploration).

3.2 Three types of relationships between exploitation and exploration

Organizational ambidexterity aims to pursue both exploitation and exploration, and thus, enable long-term growth. There are three types of relationships between exploitation and exploration.

- **Resource supply (Fig. 2 Arrow-1):** Exploitation supplies resources for exploration. It is necessary to secure resources by using existing knowledge to support exploration, in which outcomes cannot be expected in a short period.
- **Trade-off (Fig. 2 Arrow-2):** This is the trade-off around resource allocation (March, 1991; Levinthal and March, 1993; Rivkin and Siggelkow, 2003). Assuming limited resources, the more resources one obtains, the less remains for another. In allocating resources, the level of interest, awareness, and time allocated are also considered. Exploitation and exploration require different skills, and the more one skill improves, the more another degrades. Although it is desirable to attain balance, there is a general tendency to prioritize exploitation, which could bring outcomes sooner than exploration (Levitt and March, 1988; Cohen and Levinthal, 1990; Levinthal and March, 1993; Lavie and Rosenkopf, 2006).
- **Transition (Fig. 2 Arrow-3):** The role of some works is expected to change over time. When organizational learning succeeds, some promising outcomes achieved through exploration will remain and be used

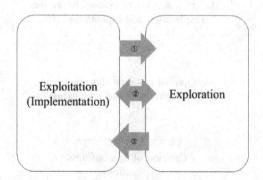

Fig. 2. Relation between exploitation and exploration.

as knowledge for the next generation (Dougherty, 1996; Sheremata, 2000; Andriopoulos and Lewis, 2009). Certain parts of the explored contents will be used in the future.

4. Problem Areas to Solve the Dematurity Strategy Issue

To avoid maturation, it is necessary to work on both operating the existing business smoothly and creating a new business. Since both exploitation and exploration are required, the role expected of management control is further complicated. The problem areas can be categorized as shown in Fig. 3.

In problem area 1, a prime consideration is the kind of management control necessary to implement the existing business efficiently. Exploratory elements, such as course correction and operational routine updates, are required to survive competition.

In problem area 2, the main agenda is about the desirable type of management control to promote business creation. In this area, the accumulated and systematized (structured) knowhow of start-up operation should offer substantial suggestions.

Problem area 3 is about the optimal resource allocation for exploration and exploitation, and the overall structural design.

When tackling the issue of dematurity strategy, the emphasis should be on problem areas 2 and 3. The next section discusses the details of each.

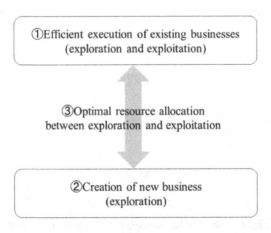

Fig. 3. Management control for the dematurity strategy.

5. Management Control for New Business Creation

What kind of management control should be exercised to create a new business efficiently? Lean start-up[4] is a well-known approach that systematized the winning patterns of start-ups in the Silicon Valley in the U.S. (Ries, 2011; 2017)

Management control for new business creation, as shown in lean start-ups, has the following five big differences from existing business operations.

1. The whole process of new business creation is a series of processes, promoting diffusion at an early stage and convergence at the last stage.
2. Real option thinking is adopted and investment does not grow at an early stage.
3. The number of trials and errors constantly increases.
4. Customers are involved in a process of scenario improvement.
5. The scenario is updated as per reality, instead of adapting reality to the original scenario.

6. Optimal Resource Allocation and Overall Structural Design

6.1 *Internal ecology model connecting exploration and exploitation*

The internal ecology model (e.g., Burgelman, 1983, 1991, 2002; Burgelman and Maidique, 1987; Burgelman *et al.*, 2006) is helpful in understanding the mutual relation between exploration (new business creation) and exploitation (existing business operation) in a company. In this model, changes in resource allocation are explained using patterns of biological evolution.

In general, the process of evolution is explained as the process of variation, selection, and retention (VSR). Variation occurs on site. Ideas leading to a new strategy (mutations) occur through autonomous trial and error

---

[4] A concept that is believed to have greatly affected lean start-up is "customer development model" (Blank, 2003).

as well as suggestions outside the scope of the originally intended strategy (implementation of the predetermined business plan = exploitation). This variation cannot be predicted accurately; however, the probability of event occurrence could be manipulated by design and operation of management control. Variation could bring choices other than the existing strategy. Most of these variations will be rejected as an official business plan by selection through an internal approval process, and will just disappear.

Some of these mutations will survive through the selection process. An example is a case in which the top management will officially approve the suggestions made by middle management, and thus, the future direction and resource allocation of the company will change accordingly. An alternative brought by variation will survive through the internal selection process and move to the retention stage, as an official business plan for implementation.

The upper part of Fig. 4 shows the process of implementing the existing business plan. Specific contents officially determined by the organization as its current strategies will be retained as a business plan. This business plan will be discussed and reviewed through the approval process.

The lower part of Fig. 4 shows the process of considering a new business plan draft. Whether any variation remains depends on whether it could be upgraded to the upper part through the processes in the lower

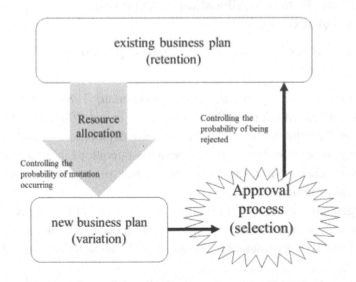

Fig. 4.   Organizational ambidexterity and management control.

part. In the approval process, a new business plan draft created through variation will be closely examined and whether it should be included in the existing business plan will be determined.

What matters here is that adjusting various management control elements could change both the probability of occurrence of a new business plan draft and the probability of such a draft surviving through the selection process. Whether it turns to a fluid pattern of many births and deaths (many variations and selections) or a stable pattern of few births and deaths (few variations and selections) depends on the design and operation of management control.

6.2 *Design of new business creation process*

This internal ecology model adjusts the probability that a new business plan draft can replace the existing business plan. Practically, a new business plan can be developed internally or procured externally. Since various methods could be adopted to design the process of new business creation, a proper one should be selected from unrestricted options.

There could be various choices for a new business plan, ranging from genuine in-house development to complete external procurement.

Roberts and Berry (1985) argue that proper approaches could be determined by the relation (sense of distance) with management resources that the current strategy relies on. Figure 5 is a matrix showing management resources in two dimensions of market knowhow and technical knowhow to illustrate the path for acquiring an optimal new business plan. If a certain level of knowhow about a given market and technology is in place, in-house development is sufficient for formulating a new business plan. In-house development with no market or technical knowhow minimizes its odds of success. In this case, external resources should be utilized.

Since there are multiple new business plans, it is reasonable to develop some parts internally and procure other parts externally. What matters is that they constitute an appropriate portfolio. It is only to be expected that a company that positively engages in in-house development may also be active in acquisition and alliance.

In recent years, many business corporations have set up funds on self-financing basis and provided funds or support (e.g., implementation of

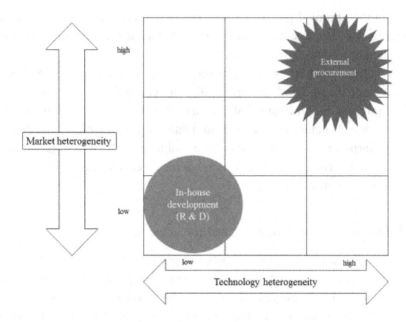

Fig. 5.   Designing the process of new business creation: In-house development vs. external procurement.

Source: Based on Roberts and Berry (1985, p. 13).

accelerator programs) to start-ups.[5] These approaches are known as corporate venture capital (CVC). What part of a new business creation process (innovation process) should be procured externally and what part should be developed internally? In case of external procurement, how and with which industry should the company become involved?

7. Conclusions

This study examines how management control can contribute to the issue of dematurity strategy. Specifically, it identifies the following three different problem areas.

The first is management control to implement the existing business efficiently. Exploration activities for new business creation do not start

---

[5] For example, Nikkei (December 14, 2017) reported that 23.2% of the surveyed companies established CVCs. If "under consideration" is included, a little more than 30% answered positively.

without first securing resources. The second is a mandatory improvement in management control within a new business. Many start-ups have achieved rapid growth, and accumulated and systematized operational knowhow, such as lean start-up. The third concerns optimal resource allocation between exploration and exploitation and the overall structural design. In particular, activities for new business creation could be performed internally and some outcomes could be procured externally. An effective mechanism is necessary to control the kind of portfolio these elements constitute, and how this portfolio is maintained.

Since its conceptualization in 1965, management control has expanded in scope by including exploration in addition to implementation. In particular, new business creation is the most difficult exploratory activity. With growing expectation of its contribution to exploration, management control is now recognized as a collection of various control tools. New business creation involves high uncertainty, making it difficult to digitize all aspects in advance accurately. Its operation needs to rely on an idea of control package. As management control now involves companies beyond individual company boundaries, the formulation of CVC or the effective use of external resources has become important in creating a new business. Desirable results could not be produced without freeing oneself from a stand-alone management mentality. The idea of a business ecosystem premised on collaboration with others has become increasingly important.

References

Abernathy, W.J. (1978). *The Productivity Dilemma*. Johns Hopkins University Press, Baltimore.

Andriopoulos, C. and Lewis, M.W. (2009). Exploitation-exploration tensions and organizational ambidexterity: Managing paradoxes of innovation, *Organization Science*, Vol. 20, No. 4, pp. 696–717.

Anthony, R. (1965). *Planning and Control Systems: A Framework for Analysis*. Division of Research, Graduate School of Business Administration, Harvard University Press, Cambridge Massachusetts.

Blank, S.G. (2003). *The Four Steps to the Epiphany: Successful Strategies for Startups That Win*, Lulu Enterprises Incorporated, Hillsborough St Raleigh, NC.

Burgelman, R.A. (1983). A model of the interaction of strategic behavior, corporate context, and the concept of strategy, *Academy of Management Review*, Vol. 8, pp. 61–70.

Burgelman, R.A. (1991). Intraorganizational ecology of strategy making and organizational adaptation: Theory and field research, *Organization Science*, Vol. 2, No. 3, pp. 239–262.

Burgelman, R.A. (2002). *Strategy Is Destiny: How Strategy-Making Shapes a Company's Future*. The Free Press, New York.

Burgelman, R.A., Grove, A.S. *et al.* (2006). *Strategic Dynamics: Concepts and Cases*. McGraw-Hill/Irwin, Boston.

Burgelman, R.A. and Maidique, M.A. (1987). *Strategic Management of Technology and Innovation*. Richard D. Irwin, Homewood Illinois.

Christensen, C.M. (1997). *The Innovator's Dilemma: When New Technologies Cause Great Firms to Fail*, Harvard Business School Press, Boston Massachusetts.

Cohen, M.W. and Levinthal, D.A. (1990). Absorptive capacity: A new perspective on learning and innovation, *Administrative Science Quarterly*, Vol. 35, No. 1, pp. 128–152.

Dougherty, D. (1996). Organizing for innovation, In S.R. Clegg, C. Hardy, *et al.*, (eds.), *Handbook of Organization Studies* (pp. 424–439). Sage Publications, Inc., Thousand Oaks California.

Hiromoto, T. (1993). *The Evolution of Management Accounting Theory*. Moriyama, Tokyo Japan.

Lavie, D. and Rosenkopf, L. (2006). Balancing exploration and exploitation in alliance formation, *Academy of Management Journal*, Vol. 49, No. 4, pp. 797–818.

Levinthal, D.A. and March, J.G. (1993). The myopia of learning, *Strategic Management Journal*, Vol. 14, pp. 95–112.

Levitt, B. and March, J.G. (1988). Organizational learning, *Annual Review of Sociology*, Vol. 14, 319–340.

March, J.G. (1991). Exploration and exploitation in organizational learning, *Organization Science*, Vol. 2, No. 1, pp. 71–87.

O'Reilly, C.A. and Tushman, M.L. (2013). Organizational ambidexterity: Past, present and future, *Academy of Management Perspectives*, Vol. 27, No. 4, pp. 324–338.

O'Reilly, C.A. and Tushman, M.L. (2016). *Lead and Disrupt: How to Solve the Innovator's Dilemma*. Stanford Business Books.

Ries, E. (2011). *The Lean Startup: How Today's Entrepreneurs Use Continuous Innovation to Create Radically Successful Businesses.* Currency.

Ries, E. (2017). *The Startup Way: How Modern Companies Use Entrepreneurial Management to Transform Culture and Drive Long-Term Growth.* Currency.

Rivkin, J.W. and Siggelkow, N. (2003). Balancing search and stability: Interdependencies among elements of organizational design, *Management Science*, Vol. 49, No. 3, pp. 290–311.

Roberts, E.B. and Berry, C.A. (1985). Entering new businesses: Selecting strategies for success, *Sloan Management Review*, Vol. 26 (Spring), pp. 3–17.

Sheremata, W.A. (2000). Centrifugal and centripetal forces in radical new product development under time pressure, *Academy of Management Review*, Vol. 25, No. 2, pp. 389–408.

Chapter 3

Segment Performance Evaluation and Asset Recycling: Case Study of a Japanese Trading Company

Makoto Tomo

Faculty of Economics, Seijo University,
Tokyo 157-8511, Japan

1. Introduction

This chapter examines the process of strategic change and the resulting change in performance evaluation indicators for Mitsui & Co. (Mitsui), a Japanese trading company. In particular, it shows that the performance evaluation index used on a company-wide or segment basis has changed from capital cost to profit/loss for the year attributable to owners of the parent, core operating cash flow (CF), and asset recycling.

This chapter consists of four parts. The first explores Mitsui's strategic change, which is also a change in the trading company business, showing the new strategy under the whole change. The second part shows profit allocation among segments, especially the investments owned by multiple segments, under the matrix management, while the third presents the changes in segment performance evaluation indicators. Mitsui has used five indicators over the last 20 years, with only two of them being used up to now, which are the profit/loss for the year attributable to owners of the parent and the core operating CF that has been used since 2014. The core operating CF is not used only as a segment performance indicator, but also in the medium-term management plan, dividend policy, and the formula of director's bonus. Fourth, it investigates "asset recycling," which Mitsui uses as a reference for investment recovery. The core operating CF and asset recycling are the sources of new investment. Regarding the asset recycling, I present examples of iron and steel products business unit (BU) and healthcare BU.

2. Strategy Change of Mitsui

2.1 *Functions of general trading companies*

Traditionally, trading companies have had trading, logistics, and financial functions; however, this pattern is changing to business investment (Asada *et al.*, 2018).

For example, Mitsui has been changing its strategy from trading to business investment over more than 20 years, which is reflected in its headquarters' total asset breakdown (Fig. 1). Out of the total assets, the ratio of investment securities and affiliated company shares has been rising for more than 20 years steadily, with the ratio being 62% in fiscal year

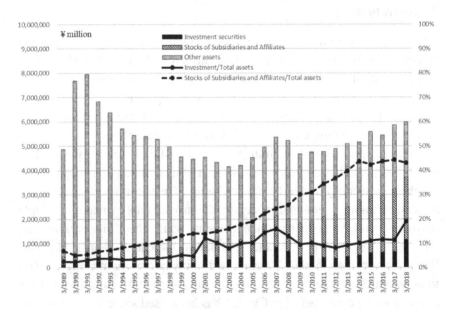

Fig. 1.   Mitsui headquarters' total asset breakdown.

Source: Mitsui & Co., *Annual Report*, 1989–2018.

(FY) 3/2018. The asset structure of Mitsui is close to that of a holding company.

2.2 Business model change of Mitsui

Looking at the operating income shown as the line plot in Fig. 2, we find that there have been deficits since FY 3/2009. In addition, looking at the bar graph after deducting the dividend income from the net income, we notice that there has been consistently a deficit since FY 3/1994. The sum of the two bar graphs shows the dividends' income, as the business model covers operating loss with the dividends' income from investment securities. Thus, Mitsui's business model has changed to carry out investment functions.

Mitsui has a heavier weight in the resource field than other trading companies, but "a shift from the resource field to a non-resource field" is also considered a strategy (Mitsui & Co., 2014), as there are business investments on the premise of selling the investment. According to the medium-term management plan announced in 2017, the strategic change of investment was adopted, with the infrastructure business switching to the "pursue, develop, and sell model" (Mitsui & Co., 2017b). This strategy

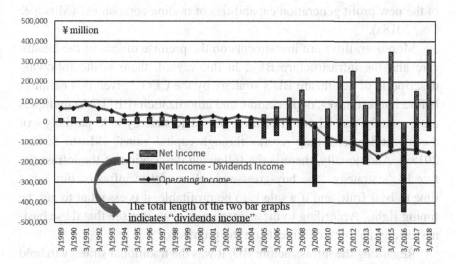

Fig. 2. Mitsui headquarters' dividend income in net income.

Source: Mitsui & Co., *Annual Report*, each year edition.

has accelerated the cycle from development to sale with respect to the power-generation business. Additionally, the healthcare business adopted the "grow & sell model" (Mitsui & Co., 2016). These models are the "asset recycling" that identify mature businesses and sell them.

Besides, there is a strategy of "acquiring fair value through profit or loss (FVTPL)" (Mitsui, 2018a), where the securities obtained from business investments are recorded as financial instruments on the balance sheet. In international financial reporting standard (IFRS) 9, financial instruments are classified into three categories: (1) amortized cost; (2) FVTPL that reflects gains and losses associated with market valuation in PL; and (3) fair value through other comprehensive income (FVOCI) that reflects gains and losses associated with market valuation in other comprehensive income.

Mitsui classifies business investments as both FVOCI and FVTPL. The FVTPL requires "financial assets held within a business model whose objective is to hold financial assets to collect contractual CFs and sell financial assets." This is exactly the case for the "buy and sell business model" of the pharmaceutical and information and communications technology (ICT) businesses. In these businesses, by classifying investment securities as FVTPL, profits arising from fair value evaluations are reflected in the net income. Therefore, Mitsui views the FVTPL as "one of the new profit generation capabilities of trading companies" (Mitsui & Co., 2018a).

Moreover, there are investments on the premise of sale of the healthcare and the infrastructure BUs. In this regard, there is the following description of healthcare BU's strategy by the CEO, "given that earnings before interest, taxes, depreciation, and amortization (EBITDA) multiples are generally very high in this area, our basic strategy is to partially exit the investment and reap returns through capital gains" (Mitsui & Co., 2018a). Additionally, there is the following description of the infrastructure BU's strategy, "the buy-grow-and-sell model in infrastructure takes time to bear fruit, and if a sale is to be profitable, it is essential to get the timing right." According to these descriptions, we can see that these businesses are making investments on the premise of sale.

Regarding the infrastructure BU, it was the traditional strategy to hold investment assets in these fields. However, there are signs of change, as

Mitsui is engaged in the business of turning solar power generation in Japan into a fund, then selling it as soon as it is completed, with the benefits already reaped. In addition, the third fund is currently being established.

3. Matrix Management and Segment Management

3.1 *Matrix management of Mitsui*

Mitsui uses a matrix organization consisting of 15 headquarters' BUs and three regional BUs, integrating the product strategies of headquarters' BUs and the regional strategies of regional BUs. According to the annual report, the roles of both are as follows. "The headquarters BUs plan overall and worldwide strategies for their products and services and conduct their worldwide operations. The BUs also collaborate with the regional BUs in planning and executing their strategies for products and regions."

The regional BUs exist in three regions: Europe, the Middle East, and Africa (EMEA), and the Americas and Asia Pacific. They manage the businesses of their regions as the centers of each particular regional strategy and operate diversified businesses together with their affiliated companies in collaboration with the headquarters' BUs. The regional BUs play the role of "local depth for global reach," which deepens the regional strategy and reaches globally. In business evaluation by segment, Mitsui treats headquarters' BUs and regional BUs equally.

3.2 *Revenue and profit/loss distribution in matrix management*

Under the matrix management, there might be an investment that belongs to both headquarters and regional BUs, thus causing a dilemma of how to distribute the profit, which Mitsui resolves using the following method. First, it determines which sector to invest in, with large-scale projects being recently more likely to be invested in by the headquarters' BUs. After the investment, the profit/loss is recorded in the investing BU. Second, when the headquarters' and regional BUs jointly invest, profit/loss is distributed according to the share of investment. For example, when the headquarters and Asia Pacific BUs invested in an Australian mining project, the profit was distributed according to the investment ratio.

In the case of indirect investments through financial subsidiaries, profit/loss is recorded not in the financial subsidiaries, but the investing BU. For example, when the headquarters' BU invested in healthcare business through the Dutch financial subsidiary, the profit/loss was recorded in the headquarters' BU, not in the EMEA (Europe) BU.

The method of profit/loss allocation for the investments jointly owned by multiple BUs has changed. Until FY 3/2015, it was distributed using non-controlling interests, with revenues being also distributed at a similar ratio. From FY 3/2016, it was distributed using the equity method (one-line consolidation), with only profit/loss being distributed, while revenue was no longer distributed. From FY 3/2018, revenues and profits have been distributed using the shareholding ratio, which is a management accounting allocation method separated from financial accounting. Regardless of which method is used, the net income of the bottom line is the same. However, if the equity method is used, revenue is not distributed. It seems that both net income and revenue that represents the scale of business are important for performance evaluation.

The aforementioned change in the profit/loss distribution method is reflected in Table 1. The adjustments and eliminations' ratio was 0% from FY 3/2013 to FY 3/2015, which was distributed using non-controlling

Table 1.   Revenue in segment information (Mitsui) (¥ billion).

	Headquarters' BUs total	Regional BUs total	Others	Adjustments and Eliminations	Consolidated total	Adjustments and Eliminations' ratio
3/2019	6,952	0	5	0	6,957	0.0%
3/2018	4,889	0	2	1	4,892	0.0%
3/2017/3*	4,362	0	2	0	4,364	0.0%
3/2017	3,528	875	8	−47	4,364	−1.1%
3/2016	3,874	930	3	−47	4,760	−1.0%
3/2015	4,362	1,041	2	0	5,405	0.0%
3/2014	4,813	917	2	0	5,732	0.0%
3/2013	4,185	725	2	0	4,912	0.0%

Note: * Reclassified based on FY 3/2018.
Source: Mitsui & Co., *Annual Report*, each year edition.

interests. In FY 3/2016 and FY 3/2017, profit/loss was distributed using the equity method, with the adjustments and eliminations' ratio being approximately 1% of the consolidated total. Applying the equity method, only profit/loss was distributed, so a certain amount of revenue might have not been distributed. After that, revenue was distributed using the shareholding ratio. As shown in Table1, the regional segment was excluded from segment information in FY 3/2018. Therefore, the adjustments and eliminations' ratio returned to 0% in FY 3/2018. Thereby, Mitsui distributes not only profit/loss, but also revenue using a management accounting method.

3.3 Profit center management for regional headquarters and its limitations

Until FY 3/2017, Mitsui treated headquarters and regional BUs equally as investment or profit centers. From FY 3/2018, Mitsui changed the category of operating segments in the segment information in the annual report, as the company's operating segments are product-operating segments comprising the headquarters' BUs, where the regional segments are consolidated by products and services. The reason was explained in the FY 3/2018 annual report as follows: "The components of deciding resources to be allocated to the segments and assessing their performance by the company's chief operating decision-maker are the components where the regional BUs were consolidated by the products and services."

In the matrix management structure, there may be overlaps in business and regions. While it is possible to manage the region as a profit center, it is difficult to manage the global "product axis." Therefore, the segment classification has changed to focus on worldwide products and services. However, the matrix management structure has not changed, with regional BUs still existing.

4. Changes in the Segment Performance Evaluation Indicators and Utilization of the Core Operating CF

4.1 Changes in the segment performance evaluation indicators

Table 2 shows changes in the segment performance evaluation indicators. Mitsui has consistently disclosed "net income/loss" or "profit/loss for the period attributable to owners of the parent" (profit after tax) as an

Table 2. Transition of accounts' titles and key performance indicators (KPIs) in the segment information.

FY 3/2018	FY 3/2015	FY 3/2014
Revenue	Revenue	Revenue
Gross profit	Gross profit	Gross profit
		Operating income (Loss)
Share of profit/loss of investments accounted for using the equity method	Share of profit of investments accounted for using the equity method	Share of profit/loss of investments accounted for using the equity method
Profit for the period attributable to owners of the parent	Profit/loss for the year attributable to owners of the parent	Profit/loss for the year attributable to owners of the parent
Total assets	Total assets	Total assets
Investments accounted for using the equity method	Investments accounted for using the equity method	Investments accounted for using the equity method
Core operating CF		
Capital additions to non-current assets	Capital additions to non-current assets	Capital additions to non-current assets
Depreciation and amortization	Depreciation and amortization	Depreciation and amortization
	EBITDA	

Notes:
Gray cells represent KPIs.
EBITDA = gross profit − selling, general and administrative expenses + dividend income + equity earnings + depreciation and amortization.
Core operating CF = operating CF increase or decrease in the working capital related CF.
Source: Mitsui & Co., *Securities Report*, FY 3/2018, 3/2015, 3/2014.

important indicator. The profit after cost of capital (PACC) is a performance evaluation indicator similar to economic value added (EVA). Mitsui stopped using PACC in 2012 for the following reasons: "the calculation of capital cost was complicated, and it was not easy for the concept of their own capital cost to fully sink in among people in the BU" (Mitsui & Co., 2012).

From FY 3/2015, EBITDA was used instead of the operating profit to measure recurring profitability. However, it was terminated in FY 3/2017, with Mitsui describing the reason as "EBITDA was judged to be not suitable as a performance evaluation index because it included impairment

Medium-term management plan   5/2014, 5/2017
Shareholder return policy   FY 3/2015 — Continued
Formula of director's bonus   FY 3/2017 — Continued
Segment information   FY 3/2018 — Continued

Fig. 3. Applying core operating CF.

Source: Mitsui & Co., *Securities Report*, each year edition.

losses at equity method affiliates." From FY 3/2018, the core operating CF has been used in place of EBITDA.

4.2 *Utilization of the core operating CF*

The core operating CF is calculated by deducting the sum of the "changes in operating assets and liabilities" from "CF from operating activities" as presented in the consolidated statements of CF. The working capital such as receivables, payables, and inventories are handled by the treasury department in Mitsui's headquarters. For this reason, CF changes within the working capital are excluded from the segment evaluation. The core operating CF is an indicator for the cash generation capacity, and simultaneously, a source of funds reallocation.

Figure 3 shows the history of using the core operating CF. First, the core operating CF appeared in the medium-term management plan "Challenge & Innovation for 2020" on May 2014. From FY 3/2015, it was used for the shareholder return policy. From FY 3/2017, it was used for the formula of the director's bonus. From FY 3/2018, it was used for the account of segment information. Thereby, the core operating CF became an important indicator for cash allocation as well as business evaluation.

4.3 *Performance-related bonus for directors and the core operating CF*

Figure 4 shows the formula for the "total amount paid in bonuses for directors." Until FY 3/2017, the formula consisted only of "consolidated profit for the period attributable to owners of the parent" (net profit). However, from FY 3/2018, the core operating CF has been incorporated into the formula, with these terms having the same weight.

FY 3/2017: Profit attributable to owners of the parent x 0.1%

FY 3/2018: (Consolidated profit for the period attributable
      to owners of the parent $\times$ 50% $\times$ 0.1%) + (Core
      operating CF $\times$ 50% $\times$ 0.1%)

Fig. 4. Formula of "total amount paid in bonuses for directors."

Source: Mitsui & Co., *Securities Report*, FY 3/2017, FY 3/2018.

5. Asset Recycling

5.1 *CF allocation and asset recycling*

As shown in Table 3, asset recycling is a major part of cash allocation along with the core operating CF. The ratio of asset recycling to cash-in was 29% in FY 3/2019. It has been around 30% over the past five years, with the amount exceeding the shareholder returns.

As for the net investment ratio (D in Table 3), excluding asset recycling from investment, it was around 50% over the past five years, with almost half of the investments made with funds from asset recycling. The net investment ratio of FY 3/2019 was 75%, the highest in the past five years, since, as will be described later, a large investment of 230 billion yen was made in the healthcare business.

5.2 *Major cases of asset recycling*

The term "asset recycling" first appeared in the investor's materials in 2007. Normally, exits from the investments are not released unless it is a very important project, since it is considered a failure. Nevertheless, in recent years, Mitsui has disclosed details of asset recycling as shown in Table 4, indicating that asset recycling is a strategic exit, not a failure (Tomo, 2019).

5.3 *Asset recycling of iron and steel products BU*

There is a case of asset recycling that transferred a part of the iron and steel business prior to the investment. Mitsui invested in Nittetsu Shoji Co. in 2002, with Nittetsu Shoji Co. becoming an equity-method affiliate. This

Table 3. Mitsui's CFs (investment and asset recycling) (¥ billion).

		3/2015	3/2016	3/2017	3/2018	3/2019
Cash Out	Investment and loans (A)	−715	−600	−635	−560	−930
	Shareholder returns	−115	−115	−145	−173	−140
Cash In	Core operating CF (B)	662	471	495	670	570
	Asset recycling (C)	340	190	290	300	230
Asset recycling ratio (D) = B/(B + C)		34%	29%	37%	31%	29%
Net investment ratio (E) = (A + C)/A		52%	68%	54%	46%	75%

Source: Mitsui & Co. (2018c, 2019), Mitsui & Co., *Annual Report*, each year edition.

Table 4. Mitsui's Asset recycling in major projects.

Results (¥ billion)	Asset recycling in major projects
FY 3/2019 ¥ 230	[Resources] Sale of its equity interest in Bengalla coal mine in Australia (thermal coal).
	[Iron & Steel Products] Transfer of business to Nippon Steel & Sumikin Bussan Corporation.
	[Lifestyle] Sale of shares in dairy manufacturing and sales company in New Zealand, sale of shares in MIMS, and sale of office building in Japan.
FY 3/2018 ¥ 300	[Resources] Recovery of loans associated with liquidation of SUMIC.
	[Energy] Partial dilution of stake in Marcellus.
	[Machinery & Infrastructure] Recovery of IPP Business loans, sale of holding in power generation operator in the UK, and sale of stake in Czech water business.
	[Iron & Steel Products] Sale of CCPS.
	[Lifestyle] Sale of buildings in Japan.
	[Innovation & Corporate Development] Sale of warehouses in Japan.
FY 3/2017 ¥ 290	[Metals] Ruyuan Sims.
	[Machinery & Infrastructure] Wind power in Australia Aircraft engines.
	[Chemicals] Chemical-related business in Brazil.
	[Energy] Tonen General Sekiyu.
	[Lifestyle] Malaysian hospital (IHH) Recruit Holdings.
	[Innovation & Corporate Development] Nihon Unisys.
	[All others/Adjustments & Eliminations] Miscellaneous.

Source: Mitsui & Co. (2019), FY 3/2019 Business Plan, Financial Results FY 3/2017.

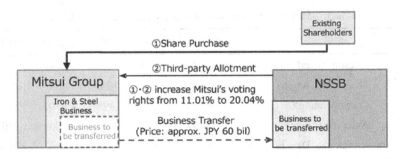

Fig. 5.　Transferring a part of the iron and steel business to NSSB.
Source: Mitsui & Co. (2017a).

was intended to support Nittetsu Shoji Co., when the steel business was in recession (Ido, 2017). Since then, the performance of Nittetsu Shoji Co. has improved and contributed to Mitsui's consolidated profits.

In 2013, Nippon Steel and Sumitomo Metal Industries merged, with their subsidiaries, Nittetsu Shoji and Sumikin Bussan, also merging with Nippon Steel & Sumikin Bussan Co. ("NSSB"). Therefore, Mitsui's share in NSSB was diluted to 11.01%, and NSSB was no longer an equity-method affiliate. Moreover, NSSB's contribution to Mitsui's consolidated profit has decreased.

As shown in Fig. 5, Mitsui transferred the partial Mitsui group's steel business to NSSB in 2018, and invested additional shares of NSSB using this fund. Thus, NSSB became an equity-method affiliate again. This case of asset recycling realized a part of the iron and steel business, and reinvested the cash gained.

5.4 *Strategy of healthcare business in healthcare BU*

As mentioned in Section 1, in the healthcare business, Mitsui is shifting its strategy from "minor investment" to "operatorship and grow & sell." The minor investment was the main strategy because Mitsui would not take risks such as hospital operation. However, under the operatorship strategy, Mitsui became deeply involved in the business operations and took risks. An investment in MicroBiopharm Japan Co. is an example of the operatorship strategy. After acquiring the pharmaceutical division of

Mercian Corporation in 2011, Mitsui dispatched management and implemented a "profit management and sales reform" to improve profitability.

The "grow & sell" strategy is to invest in growth areas, then recover investment through asset recycling and invest the fund in the next growth areas (Mitsui & Co., 2016). An investment in the Malaysian hospital IHH Healthcare Berhad (IHH) is an example of the "grow & sell" strategy. Mitsui acquired 30% share of IHH for 92.4 billion yen in 2011. After that, Mitsui's share decreased to 20.1% due to acquisition by IHH and listing on IHH. In September 2016, Mitsui sold 2% of the issued shares, collecting 24.9 billion yen in cash and gaining a profit of 14.6 billion yen. Mitsui invested in the healthcare business in the United States and India using the funds gained. The market capitalization of the IHH stake before the 2% sell was about 250 billion yen, being almost three times the initial investment.

Mitsui acquired an additional 16% share of IHH for 230 billion yen in March 2019, raising its share to 32.9% with this deal and becoming the largest shareholder. The cumulative amount of the investment in IHH is estimated to be around 300 billion yen after subtracting the amount recovered so far.

Compared to the annual total investment in the last 5 years, which was 500–900 billion yen, this was a large-scale investment equivalent to about 25–50% of the total investment. The investment in IHH was of a size that required corrections to the CF allocation in the medium-term management plan. Looking at the corrections shown in Table 5, investment has increased by 200 billion yen, with asset recycling also increasing by 100 billion yen. Therefore, we can see that funds are raised by simultaneously conducting asset recycling and investment. Additionally, we can see that Mitsui is implementing the "grow & sell" strategy using asset recycling.

Investing in IHH was part of a strategy to build an ecosystem in the healthcare field and simultaneously harvest the surrounding areas. Mitsui has been implementing the operatorship strategy that supports IHH's business expansion through initial public offering (IPO), overseas mergers and acquisitions (M&A), and management participation through director dispatching and seconding.

Table 5. Revised CF allocation in the medium-term management plan (¥ billion).

		3-year cumulative (Announced in Oct/2018) (FY 3/2018–FY 3/2020)	3-year cumulative (Current revision) (FY 3/2018–FY 3/2020)
Cash In	Core operating CF	1,900	1,900
	Asset recycling	700	800
Cash Out	Investment and loans	−1,700 to −1,900	−1,900 to −2,100
	Shareholder returns	−410	−450
Free CF after shareholder returns		290–490	150–350

Source: Mitsui & Co. (2018b).

6. Conclusion and Further Challenges

Section 2 shows the changes in business in a trading company, as the main focus of general trading companies has shifted from trading to business investment. Mitsui was implementing a "buy, grow, & sell" strategy in the IT and healthcare businesses. By classifying these investment assets as FVTPL, changes in fair value are reflected in the net income, and Mitsui was considering making this one of the main profit sources.

In Section 3, I analyze the matrix management and segment management of Mitsui. The method of distributing revenues and profits between segments has changed from the equity method to the shareholding ratio. Besides, Mitsui changed its decision-making and performance evaluation from FY 3/2018 to a business model that integrated regional BUs with headquarters' BUs.

Section 4 analyzes the transition of Mitsui's segment performance indicators. Mitsui has used indicators such as profit after tax, operating profit, PACC, core operating CF, and EBITDA over the past 20 years. Mitsui used PACC with capital costs from 2004 to around 2012. EBITDA was used only for 3 years from FY 3/2015. Since FY 3/2018, Mitsui has focused on two performance evaluation indicators, namely, profit after tax and the core operating CF. The core operating CF is also used as a formula for dividend policy and performance-based compensation for directors.

Section 5 analyzes asset recycling through cases in the iron and steel and healthcare businesses. Mitsui has adopted a "grow & sell" strategy to reinvest in the next growth area while recovering investment through asset recycling.

As described above, Mitsui had changed its performance evaluation indicators from capital cost to CF-based to reap the fruits of investment as cash, and replace the business investment portfolio with growth areas. As the strategy changes, the management control system that supports it has to be flexibly changed as well.

Portfolio management is also carried out at other trading and general business companies. Furthermore, Mitsubishi Corporation has a strategy equivalent to Mitsui's asset recycling called "peak out." Future research should further study whether changes in performance indicators are occurring in these companies.

References

Asada Takayuki, Tomo Makoto *et al.* (2018). Corporate management evolution and management accounting issues in ASEAN cluster. *Accounting* (Chuokeizai-sha), Vol. 70, No. 6, pp. 112–117. (In Japanese.)

Ido Seiichi, (2017). Mitsui's successful strategy for acquiring Japan's largest steel trading company, *Economist* (Mainichi Shimbun Publishing), Vol. 95, No. 41, p. 111. (In Japanese.)

Mitsui & Co. *Annual Report*, each year editions.

Mitsui & Co. *Securities Report*, each year editions.

Mitsui & Co. (2012). IR Meeting on financial results for the year ended March 31, 2012, questions and answers, (May 8, 2012). (https://www.mitsui.com/jp/en/ir/library/meeting/__icsFiles/afieldfile/2015/07/21/en_123_4q_qa_1.pdf).

Mitsui & Co. (2014). IR meeting on new medium-term management plan questions and answers, (May 8, 2014). (https://www.mitsui.com/jp/en/ir/library/meeting/__icsFiles/afieldfile/2015/07/21/en_143_4q_chukei_qa.pdf).

Mitsui & Co. (2016). Healthcare BU business briefing (for reporters), (December 1, 2016). (In Japanese.) (https://www.mitsui.com/jp/ja/ir/meeting/management/__icsFiles/afieldfile/2016/12/21/ja_161201_ppt.pdf).

Mitsui & Co. (2017a). Transferring a part of the iron and steel products business of the Mitsui group to NSSB and additional acquisition of the shares in NSSB, (October 4, 2017). (https://www.mitsui.com/jp/en/release/2017/__icsFiles/afieldfile/2017/10/04/en_171004_attach.pdf).

Mitsui & Co. (2017b). Investor day 2017, Machinery & Infrastructure presentation material, (June 6, 2017). (https://www.mitsui.com/jp/en/ir/meeting/investorday/2017/pdf/3_machinery_infrastracture.pdf).

Mitsui & Co. (2018a). 2nd quarter financial results announcement for FY ending March 2019 QA Session, (October 31, 2018). (https://www.mitsui.com/jp/en/ir/library/meeting/__icsFiles/afieldfile/2018/11/06/en_181031_meeting_qa.pdf).

Mitsui & Co. (2018b). Acquisition of additional shares of IHH Healthcare Berhad (IHH), Asia's largest private hospital group, (November 29, 2018). (https://www.mitsui.com/jp/en/release/2018/__icsFiles/afieldfile/2018/11/29/en_181129_Paramount_attach_2.pdf).

Mitsui & Co. (2018c). Progress of medium-term management plan and FY Mar/2019 business plan, (May 8, 2018). (http://www.irwebcasting.com/20180509/7/9c4a84db44/media/180509_mitsuiandco_en.pdf).

Mitsui & Co. (2019). Progress of medium-term management plan and FY Mar/2020 business plan, (April 26, 2019). (https://www.irwebcasting.com/20190509/2/2286dc6473/media/en_193_4q_ppt.pdf).

Tomo Makoto, (2019). Intercultural management and management accounting issues: From case studies of pure holding companies and Japanese overseas subsidiaries, *The Journal of Management Accounting*, Vol. 27, No. 2, pp. 13–26. (In Japanese.)

Chapter 4

Financial Information Analysis for Business Portfolio Strategy: With Reference to Segment Reporting by Mitsubishi Electric Group

Shufuku Hiraoka

Faculty of Business Administration, Soka University,
Tokyo 192-8577, Japan

1. Introduction

An important corporate strategy issue is the formulation of a business portfolio strategy that enables continuation and growth of the corporate group. Business portfolio strategy could also be said to represent the management's accountability vis-à-vis their company's stakeholders, most notably its investors. At the same time as analyzing their group's current situation and then obtaining stakeholders' approval of the results of strategic formulation arising from this analysis, the top management of each corporate group must give an indication of overall strategic direction to those involved in each of the group's segments. There is truth in the idea that financial information produced in accordance with the criterion for reporting segment classification known as "management approach" is potentially helpful for both of these aims (Solomons, 1968; Hiraoka, 2010). This study analyzes information on segments for each type of business in the Mitsubishi Electric Group; these segments are formulated in accordance with the management approach. The study also aims to make suggestions regarding strategic management control in which a company's top management formulates business portfolio strategy while remaining aware of the stakeholders and brings together those involved in the company's internal segments (Hiraoka, 2019).

2. Survey of Previous Research

This study analyzes business segment information to obtain suggestions on how such information can support formulation of business portfolio strategy. The author has already published similar studies over a number of years (e.g., Hiraoka, 2010). However, there has been an insufficient number of such studies that also incorporate appraisal of risk.

Monden (1980) was one of the first to clarify the relationship between Boston Consulting Group's product portfolio management (PPM) and segment information and, in a study that extended this idea, he combined the capital asset pricing model from finance theory with the existing PPM model, thereby incorporating a means of risk measurement within business evaluation. This idea had already been proposed by others, including Rabino and Wright (1984), but Monden and Fernand (1995) added the risk measurement to Boston Consulting Group's two-dimensional PPM and they made a new original three-dimensional PPM. In other words, they converted the quadrant of business classification from $2 \times 2 = 4$ to $2 \times 2 \times 2 = 8$ by adding the risk measurement to Boston Consulting Group's PPM.

The PPM method was also extended in various other ways and, as it incorporated qualitative evaluation and came to reflect both the limitations of analysis-based strategic management and the increasing emphasis on process-based strategic management, its status as a strategic method remained within the domain of traditional research.

Despite this, it is clear that business portfolio strategy occupies an important role within overall corporate strategy. This is evident during observation of the strategic failure of electrical appliance groups that, forgetting their origins, have struggled for many years, and of their rebirth (Hiraoka, 2014, 2016). For example, Sony recently divided a wide range of business fields into three areas, namely (1) "market stimulation," (2) "stable earnings," and (3) "business change risk control," setting out the strategic direction for each area (Sony's Annual Securities Report, 2016). Hiraoka (2017) also deals with strategic positioning based on such PPM-based concepts and their contribution to synergy between businesses and to the corporate group as a whole.

3. Selection of Research Subject and Data Collection Source

The subject of this research is the segment data for Mitsubishi Electric Group produced by the redivision of data in its consolidated financial statements according to the type of business. This set of data was selected because, as it belongs to an electrical appliance group rather than a specialist company, it was appropriately diverse and given that reporting segment classification remained unchanged from the March 2001 financial year (FY3/01) to the March 2018 financial year (FY3/18), it was easy to carry out time series analysis of profitability, growth, risk evaluation, and cash flow. Data were collected from the information platform Nikkei Value Search, with the cooperation of Nikkei Media Marketing, Inc. From this source, as well as the Mitsubishi Electric Group segment data, data related to 10-year Japanese government bond yields from FY3/01 to FY3/18 were obtained.

4. Analysis of Segment Information for Each Type of Business

4.1 *Reporting segments (types of businesses)*

Reporting segments for each type of business in the Mitsubishi Electric Group covered by this study are as follows.

- Energy and electric systems
- Industry automation systems
- Information and communication systems
- Electronic devices
- Home appliances
- Other

4.2 Calculation of return on assets and cash flow return on assets for the reporting segments

Segment data were used to calculate return on assets (ROA) and cash flow return on assets (CFROA) for the reporting segments. The following formulas were used to calculate ROA and CFROA.

$$ROA = \frac{\text{Operating profit}}{(\text{Assets at term start} + \text{assets at term end}) \div 2} \times 100$$

$$CFROA = \frac{\text{Operating profit} \times (1 - \text{legal effective tax rate}) + \text{depreciation}}{(\text{Assets at term start} + \text{assets at term end}) \div 2} \times 100$$

4.3 Relationship between reporting segment ROA and CFROA and consolidated earnings

Here, correlation coefficients are used to clarify the relationship between reporting segment ROA and CFROA and consolidated earnings (after consolidated elimination). ROA and CFROA correlation coefficients based on simple totals before elimination of transactions between reporting segments were also calculated (see Tables 1 and 2). It should be noted that, when considering the synergy between businesses, the correlation coefficient between reporting segments is important, and this problem is touched upon in Section 4.8.

Table 1. ROA correlation coefficients.

Reporting segments	Based on simple total	After consolidation elimination
Energy and electric systems	0.14	0.13
Industrial automation systems	0.62	0.63
Information and communication systems	0.78	0.77
Electronic devices	0.69	0.7
Home appliances	0.48	0.49
Other	0.85	0.84

Table 2. CFROA correlation coefficients.

Reporting segments	Based on simple total	After consolidation elimination
Energy and electric systems	0.09	0.30
Industrial automation systems	0.72	0.63
Information and communication systems	0.35	0.64
Electronic devices	0.66	0.69
Home appliances	0.73	0.76
Other	0.53	0.46

The resulting coefficients are used as an element in the calculation of the following indicator termed the "business β," which shows the evaluated risk of each reporting segment.

4.4 *Evaluation of ROA and CFROA risk for each reporting segment: Calculation of "business β"*

Here, β is the sensitivity of how the change of profitability of a certain business segment will vary depending on the changes of total profitability of the whole portfolio of the segments of the consolidated corporate group as a whole. In other words, β is a value that corresponds to the product β concept advocated by Rabino and Wright (1984) and is calculated using the following formula:

$$\text{Business } \beta = r_{ip}\sigma_i\,\sigma_p\,/\,(\sigma_p)^2$$

where r_{ip} represents correlation coefficient of rate of return for the entire business portfolio and rate of return for the reporting segment, σ_i represents standard deviation of the rate of return for reporting segment i, and σ_p represents standard deviation of the rate of return for the whole business portfolio.

Rate of return is either ROA or CFROA, and rate of return for the entire business portfolio refers to rate of return based on simple totals of relevant figures for each segment and rate of return after consolidation elimination,

Table 3. ROA business β and risk evaluation.

Reporting segments	Based on simple total	After consolidation elimination	Risk
Energy and electric systems	0.096625044	0.08827027	Very low
Industrial automation systems	0.855406016	0.886649513	Slightly low
Information and communication systems	1.198909373	1.207607615	High
Electronic devices	2.693706561	2.775487714	Very high
Home appliances	0.406565359	0.430043979	Low
Other	0.991356461	1.011225358	Slightly high

Table 4. CFROA business β and risk evaluation.

Reporting segments	Based on simple total	After consolidation elimination	Risk
Energy and electric systems	0.047258867	0.246378561	Very low
Industrial automation systems	0.694927193	0.984910671	Slightly low
Information and communication systems	0.432821181	1.280489067	High
Electronic devices	1.747189088	2.976219218	Very high
Home appliances	0.481594123	0.808305167	Low
Other	0.460824973	0.652100435	Low

as described in Section 4.3. Table 3 shows business β when rate of return is taken to be ROA and relevant risk evaluation, and Table 4 shows business β when rate of return is taken to be CFROA and relevant risk evaluation.

There are six levels of risk evaluation: "very high," "high," "slightly high," "slightly low," "low," and "very low." As can be understood from these results, risk distribution in the Mitsubishi Electric Group is well balanced. That said, "risk" signifies the degree of sensitivity of the rate of return for each reporting segment to the group's average rate of return based on simple totals and to the group's average rate after consolidation elimination.

4.5 *Reporting segment growth analysis*

Here, the rate of growth in sales in each reporting segment is used as an indicator of its growth (Table 5). The Boston Consulting Group model

Table 5. The rate of growth in sales of reporting segments FY3/02–FY3/18.

Fiscal year (term ending March)	Energy and electric systems	Industrial automation systems	Information and communication systems	Electronic devices	Home appliances	Other	Based on simple total	After consolidation elimination
2018	1.1	10.3	-2.6	8.4	4.5	7.1	5.1	4.5
2017	-2.9	-0.9	-20.2	-11.8	2.3	0.8	-3.1	-3.5
2016	2.9	3.1	0.3	-11.3	3.9	-4.4	1.1	1.6
2015	4.1	16.7	2	22.5	0.1	9.5	7.6	6.6
2014	11.5	18.4	5	18.6	15	14.5	13.7	13.7
2013	3	-5.2	1.2	-18.3	-3.3	-3.5	-2.4	-2
2012	-0.1	5.5	5.8	14.1	-8.1	0.4	0.7	-0.2
2011	-1.1	26.4	-7.3	26.6	12.1	10.2	8.8	8.7
2010	-0.4	-13.9	-9.6	-16.8	-9.9	-7.2	-8.2	-8.5
2009	-1.4	-16.3	-9.7	-13.1	-8.5	-9.8	-9.1	-9.5
2008	11.2	6.3	-6.3	3.3	8.5	4.8	5.5	5
2007	9.5	11.3	6.78	9.1	2.8	4.5	7.2	7
2006	9.7	10	4.9	3.7	3.5	3.8	6.4	5.7
2005	-0.7	10.2	-9.9	-3.6	10.8	14.4	4.1	3.1
2004	-7.4	11	-0.7	-63	-0.9	-10.2	-8.8	-9.1
2003	-6.5	6.5	-10	-2.1	8.7	-0.6	-1.2	-0.3
2002	1.1	-9.4	-18.4	-34.2	-0.9	-5	-11	-11.6
Average	2.0	5.3	-4.0	-4.0	2.4	1.7	1.0	0.7
Distribution	32.6	130.9	68.0	492.3	53.0	61.2	52.5	52.2
Standard deviation	5.7	11.4	8.2	22.2	7.3	7.8	7.2	7.2
Average in most recent 5yrs	3.34	9.52	-3.1	5.28	5.16	5.5	4.88	4.58

Table 6. Trends in reporting segment sales composition (%).

Fiscal year(term ending March)	Energy and electric systems	Industrial automation systems	Information and communication systems	Electronic devices	Home appliances	Other
2001	19.99	14.55	20.52	15.68	16.09	13.17
2002	22.73	14.83	18.83	11.61	17.93	14.07
2003	21.51	15.97	17.15	11.50	19.71	14.15
2004	21.85	19.44	18.68	4.67	21.43	13.93
2005	20.84	20.57	16.16	4.33	22.80	15.31
2006	21.49	21.27	15.93	4.21	22.17	14.93
2007	21.94	22.08	15.87	4.29	21.27	14.55
2008	23.13	22.25	14.09	4.20	21.87	14.45
2009	25.11	20.49	14.01	4.02	22.03	14.34
2010	27.25	19.21	13.79	3.64	21.61	14.49
2011	24.75	22.32	11.75	4.24	22.26	14.68
2012	24.55	23.39	12.34	4.80	20.30	14.62
2013	25.91	22.72	12.79	4.02	20.11	14.45
2014	25.42	23.67	11.81	4.19	20.34	14.56
2015	24.60	25.68	11.20	4.77	18.92	14.83
2016	25.05	26.18	11.11	4.19	19.45	14.02
2017	25.11	26.79	9.16	3.81	20.54	14.59
2018	24.17	28.12	8.49	3.94	20.42	14.87

uses the rate of growth in the market. However, reporting segment classification is specific to Mitsubishi Electric Group's strategy and, because each segment includes a diverse range of products, determining a relevant rate of market growth would be problematic.

For the "average," it is not only the average value from FY3/02 to FY3/18 that is used. As can be seen in Table 6, sales composition changed significantly over the 18-year period and the average value for the most recent five years is therefore also included in Table 5.

4.6 *Reporting segment profitability variance analysis*

Variance in profitability signifies the difference between actual rate of return of each reporting segment and its required rate of return (RRR). RRR is obtained using business β, the risk-free rate, and the average rate of return for the entire business portfolio (based both on simple totals of data for each reporting segment and data after consolidation elimination); the risk-free rate is around 1%, which is the average value of the 10-year Japanese government bond yield from FY3/02 to FY3/18.

When the risk-free rate is Rf and the actual rate of return is the actual average rate of return from FY2/02 to FY3/18, variance in profitability can be calculated using the following formulas:

RRR = Rf + business β × (average rate of return for the whole business portfolio – Rf)

Variance in profitability = actual rate of return less RRR

The underlined section is the average excess rate of return (either on a simple-total or a consolidated basis) and indicates the risk premium. Thus, when the RRR for a reporting segment is the same as the average group-wide rate of return either on a simple-total or consolidated basis, the business β of that reporting segment is 1.0. If the variance in profitability is positive, the variance is favorable; if it is negative, the variance is unfavorable.

For example, taking the entire business portfolio to be a simple total of all reporting segments, when the rate of return is taken to be ROA, the indicators for the energy and electric systems business can be calculated as follows:

Energy and electric systems business RRR
= 1% + 0.096625044 × (5.9% – 1%) = 1.5%

Energy and electric systems business profitability variance
= 5.4% – 1.5% = 3.9% (favorable variance)

Similarly, when taking the entire business portfolio to be the relevant consolidated figure, and the rate of return to be CFROA, the indicators for the information and communication systems business can be calculated as follows:

Information and communication systems
business RRR = 1% + 1.207607615 × (5.2% − 1%) = 6%

Information and communication systems business
profitability variance = 1.6% − 6% = −4.4%
(unfavorable variance)

Tables 7 and 8 list the RRR, the actual rate of return, and the profitability variance for all reporting segments on a simple-total basis and a consolidated basis.

Table 7. Profitability variance based on ROA.

| | Rate of return | | | | | |
| | (Simple total)(%) | | | (Consolidated)(%) | | |
Reporting segments	**RRR**	**Act.**	**Var.**	**RRR**	**Act.**	**Var.**
Energy and electric systems	1.5	5.4	3.9	1.4	5.4	4.0
Industrial automation systems	5.2	11.8	6.6	4.7	11.8	7.2
Information and communication systems	6.9	1.6	−5.3	6.0	1.6	−4.4
Electronic devices	14.2	1.5	−12.7	12.5	1.5	−11.0
Home appliances	3.0	5.2	2.2	3.7	5.2	1.6
Other	5.9	6.8	0.9	7.2	6.8	−0.5

Table 8. Profitability variance based on CFROA.

| | Rate of return | | | | | |
| | (Simple total)(%) | | | (Consolidated)(%) | | |
Reporting segments	**RRR**	**Act.**	**Var.**	**RRR**	**Act.**	**Var.**
Energy and electric systems	1.3	5.4	4.0	2.6	5.4	2.8
Industrial automation systems	5.6	13.2	7.6	7.4	13.2	5.8
Information and communication systems	3.9	6.0	2.1	9.4	6.0	−3.3
Electronic devices	12.7	11.0	−1.7	20.4	11.0	−9.4
Home appliances	4.2	7.4	3.1	6.3	7.4	1.1
Other	4.1	7.8	3.8	5.3	7.8	2.6

Looking at these calculations, it is clear that variance is often unfavorable for reporting segments evaluated as "high" or "very high" risk in the business β risk evaluation in Tables 3 and 4. It is also clear that variance is lower for CFROA than for ROA in the consolidated data for all reporting segments apart from the "other" segment (here, the FY3/02–FY3/18 average on a simple-total and a consolidated basis is used for the business portfolio rate of return).

4.7 *Reporting segment approximated FCF analysis*

Working capital per segment is not disclosed in the segment information. Thus, the following formula is used for the CFROA denominator. In this study, this is defined as approximated operating cash flow.

Approximated operating CF
= operating profit × (1 − legal effective tax rate) + depreciation

Furthermore, capital expenditure for each segment is disclosed and approximated operating cash flow less capital expenditure is therefore taken to be approximated free cash flow (FCF).

Approximated FCF = approximated operating CF − capital expenditure

When this indicator is positive, this signifies that when sales growth in a particular reporting segment leads to an increase in working capital in that segment and there is a surplus after reinvestment in that segment, that surplus can be used for wider purposes including investment in other segments with insufficient capital, repayment of company-level borrowing, redemption of corporate bonds, share buyback, or dividend payment. When approximated FCF is negative in a reporting segment, this signifies a capital deficit in that segment so that, while also evaluating the segment's contribution in terms of transactions and synergy with other segments, it is necessary to make decisions as to whether to commit additional capital or to refrain from investment, and as to how to obtain a systematic return on existing investment.

Table 9 shows approximated FCF for each of Mitsubishi Electric Group's reporting segments, a simple total of approximated FCF for all segments, and the relevant consolidated figure for FY3/01 to FY3/18.

Table 9. Approximated FCF for reporting segments (yen million).

Fiscal year (term ending March)	Energy and electric systems	Industrial automation systems	Information and communication systems	Electronic devices	Home appliances	Other	Based on simple total	After consolidation elimination
2018	34,942	118,543	8,741	7,022	38,819	5,532	213,599	192,626
2017	23,108	94,599	9,603	10,662	39,464	6,969	184,405	164,892
2016	21,251	95,236	6,017	10,980	35,150	17,311	185,945	167,403
2015	40,285	8,357	17,643	7,104	1,028	13,173	180,290	162,256
2014	42,534	49,530	2,545	7,464	31,198	9,787	143,058	126,015
2013	39,612	28,220	6,049	-5,619	9,918	11,130	89,310	72,113
2012	44,199	46,596	19,494	-8,102	4,709	11,865	118,762	102,082
2011	47,496	63,257	12,108	-1,234	20,926	10,833	153,386	138,335
2010	45,248	27,235	20,331	-10,717	335	2,543	84,976	69,573
2009	43,925	27,842	29,047	-22,787	18,036	7,989	104,051	88,208
2008	27,640	67,808	16,427	-1,722	38,466	11,001	159,620	143,571
2007	27,740	70,501	9,922	9,022	17,683	8,703	143,570	127,468
2006	11,304	58,398	9,541	8,299	3,416	5,777	96,735	81,364
2005	19,931	31,846	-1,585	5,114	3,343	8,650	67,299	54,008
2004	20,515	37,038	4,022	957	15,091	5,860	83,483	69,899
2003	35,496	35,931	-6,555	15,736	29,001	19,026	128,634	116,151
2002	25,236	10,703	-53,971	-35,869	23,971	15,419	-14,511	-27,903
2001	23,351	28,877	-25,941	7,301	20,523	9,081	63,191	51,939
Average	31,698	45,998	4,394	-201	18,368	10,301	116,012	100,434
Standard deviation	11,217	25,815	19,437	13,324	13,218	4,239	52,503	50,973

Financial Information Analysis for Business Portfolio Strategy 63

Looking at these data, it is clear that, in some years, negative cash flow occurred in reporting segments appraised as "high risk" or "very high risk."

4.8 Overall evaluation of the business in each reporting segment: Strategic positioning within the group

This subsection presents an overall evaluation of the business of each reporting segment and its strategic positioning within the group is clarified. As well as the analysis of profitability, approximated FCF, growth (rate of growth in sales), risk (Tables 10 and 11), and sales composition ranking, which have already been discussed, overall business evaluation includes the degree of contribution to other reporting segments (as represented by the weighting of internal sales within the segment's total sales) and the correlation coefficients of profitability indicators between reporting segments (Tables 12–14).

* *Energy and electric systems*: On a 17-year average basis, the segment ranks 3rd in terms of ROA and 6th in terms of CFROA and does not therefore seem to contribute to profitability at first glance. However, it

Table 10. Business evaluation of reporting segments according to profitability and approximated FCF.

| | Profitability | | | | | | Approximated FCF (Avg.) million yen | | | |
| | ROA(17-yr avg%) | | | CFROA(17-yr avg%) | | | 17-yr | | Last 5-yr | |
Reporting segments	%	Rank	Evaluation	%	Rank	Evaluation	Value	Rank	Value	Rank
Energy and electric systems	5.4	③	Medium	5.4	⑥	Medium	31,700	②	32,400	②
Industrial automation systems	11.8	①	High	13.2	①	High	46,000	①	73,300	①
Information and communication systems	1.6	⑤	Low	6.0	⑤	Medium	4,400	⑤	8,900	⑤
Electronic devices	1.5	⑥	Low	11.0	②	High	–200	⑥	8,600	⑥
Home appliances	5.2	④	Medium	7.4	④	Medium	18,400	③	29,100	③
Other	6.8	②	Medium	7.8	③	Medium	10,300	④	10,600	④

Table 11. Business evaluation of reporting segments according to growth and risk.

| Reporting segments | Sales growth rate(%) | | | | Risk (business β) | | | |
| | 17-yr avg. | Last 5-yr avg. | Rank | Value | ROA | | CFROA | |
					Rank	Evaluation	Rank	Evaluation
Energy and electric systems	2.0	3.3	⑤	Medium	①	Very low	①	Very low
Industrial automation systems	5.3	9.5	①	High	③	Slightly low	④	Slightly low
Information and communication systems	−4.0	−3.1	⑥	Negative	⑤	High	⑤	High
Electronic devices	−4.0	5.3	③	Medium	⑥	Very High	⑥	Very High
Home appliances	2.4	5.2	④	Medium	②	Low	③	Low
Other	1.7	5.5	②	Medium	④	Slightly High	②	Low

Table 12. Sales composition ranking and internal sales weighting for each reporting segment.

| Reporting segments | Sales composition ranking | | Internal sales as % of segment sales | |
	FY 3/01	FY 3/18	FY 3/01	FY 3/18
Energy and electric systems	②	②	1.2%	0.7%
Industrial automation systems	⑤	①	1.3%	0.9%
Information and communication systems	①	⑤	0.7%	10.8%
Electronic devices	④	⑥	8.6%	18.2%
Home appliances	③	③	1.0%	1.5%
Other	⑥	④	55.1%	76.7%
			10.3%	13.8%

Table 13. Coefficient of ROA between reporting segments.

Reporting segments	ROA correlation coefficient					
	Energy and electric systems	Industrial automation systems	Information and communication systems	Electronic devices	Home appliances	Other
Energy and electric systems	1.000	−0.382	0.124	−0.297	−0.011	0.322
Industrial automation systems		1.000	0.247	0.769	0.518	0.401
Information and communication systems			1.000	0.369	−0.036	0.572
Electronic devices				1.000	0.330	0.444
Home appliances					1.000	0.511
Other						1.000

Table 14. Coefficient of CFROA correlation between reporting segments.

Reporting segments	CFROA correlation coefficient					
	Energy and electric systems	Industrial automation systems	Information and communication systems	Electronic devices	Home appliances	Other
Energy and electric systems	1.000	−0.441	0.328	−0.157	0.037	0.482
Industrial automation systems		1.000	0.151	0.785	0.602	0.178
Information and communication systems			1.000	0.251	0.149	−0.092
Electronic devices				1.000	0.511	0.146
Home appliances					1.000	0.556
Other						1.000

ranks 2nd in terms of approximated FCF on both a 17-year average and a most-recent-five-year average basis and it does not rank very high in terms of sales growth (5th position), making it a stable very low-risk business. It has a modest negative correlation with the industrial automation segment, but in terms of CFROA it has a modest positive correlation with information and communication systems and "other." In terms of weighting within total sales (sales composition), the segment ranks 2nd in both FY3/01 and FY3/18, meaning that it can in essence be considered a stable, cash-generating business area.

- *Industrial automation systems*: This segment ranks top in terms of profitability, approximated FCF, and sales growth and is therefore the top-earning star business. It is also lower than the group average in terms of risk. In terms of profitability, apart from a modest negative correlation with the energy and electrical systems segment, it has a positive correlation with all business areas. There is relatively high positive correlation with the electronic device and home appliance businesses.

- *Information and communication systems*: Looking at profitability, the segment ranks 5th in terms of both ROA and CFROA, its sales growth is negative, and only the electronic device segment has higher risk. Thus, the segment appears to have a low degree of contribution in terms of profitability, growth, and risk. However, its average approximated FCF is not negative and has improved such that the most-recent-five-year average is double the 17-year average. The segment ranked top in terms of sales composition in FY3/01 but had fallen to 5th in FY3/18 because of transformation of the structure of the industry. However, the weighting of internal sales within the segment's total sales has increased sharply (from 0.7% in FY3/01 to 10.8% in FY3/18), and it mostly has a slight positive correlation with other business areas in terms of profitability; where the correlation is negative, the coefficient is so low that the segments can be considered uncorrelated. It can be said that the information and communication systems segment should also be appreciated for its contribution to other business areas.

- *Electronic devices*: The segment ranks bottom (sixth) in profitability in terms of 17-year average ROA, but has the capacity to effectively generate cash flow through operations, ranking 2nd in terms of 17-year average CFROA. Most-recent-five-year average approximated FCF is positive. However, risk is very high, with the segment ranking sixth on this metric. In terms of sales composition, the segment fell from fourth position to sixth (bottom), but the weighting of internal sales within the segment's total sales rose sharply (from 8.6% in FY3/01 to 18.2% in FY3/18), and its profitability has positive correlation with that in other reporting segments (coefficient of correlation of ROA with that of industrial automation systems 0.769, information and communication systems 0.369, home appliances 0.330, and "other" 0.444; coefficient of correlation of CFROA with that of industrial automation systems 0.785, information and communication systems 0.251, and home appliances 0.511). Given this, it can be said that, as with the information and communication system segment, the electronic device segment should be appreciated for its contribution to other business areas.

- *Home appliances*: Whereas the segment ranks fourth in terms of 17-year average ROA and CFROA and third in terms of 17-year average and most-recent-five-year average approximated FCF, it is probably safe to say that, having mid-range sales growth and low risk, it is second only to energy and electric systems in being a stable, cash-generating business. Sales composition ranking was the same in FY3/01 and FY3/18, third, and the weighting of internal sales within the segment's total sales is low. However, it has positive correlation with other segments (notably with industrial automation systems and electronic devices), and it is probably true to say that, in this respect too, it is an important stable business area.

- *Other*: As the segment is mid-ranked in terms of profitability, fourth in terms of approximated FCF, and second in terms of growth, it is possible that this segment includes businesses with potential. The weighting of internal sales within the segment's total sales is very high, there is high positive ROA correlation with that of all other segments, and the positive correlation of CFROA with that of energy and electric systems and home appliances is also high.

5. Business Portfolio Strategy Support

The "management approach" is now being adopted as a criterion for segment classification of segment information for each type of business. The intention is for external reporting to be an extension of management accounting information. That is, relevant materials must have the function of allowing stakeholders, especially investors, to make judgments on corporate group performance and strategic direction from the same viewpoint as management, to a certain extent. Because management ensures stakeholders understand these things, the approach also has the function of achieving management accountability with regard to business portfolio strategy and relevant performance (Hiraoka, 2017).

In the process of establishing reporting segments, management must also first bear in mind conformance with business portfolio strategy and, if the businesses to be included in each reporting segment are bundled together on that assumption, then surely their accounting information will also function as management accounting information for corporate strategy.

In formulating business portfolio strategy, with a view to corporate sustainability and growth, the strategic positioning of each business area handled by the corporate group is clarified, and optimal company-wide resource allocation is determined. Capturing the current state of a business area's performance in management accounting information reveals its strategic positioning and, if any variance between actual performance and the required performance criteria (and the factors underlying this variance) can be identified, this knowledge can be used as business area performance management information in the pursuance of strategic management control. As previously mentioned, such analysis of segment information for each type of business can also be seen as a starting point for support of their business portfolio strategy.

6. Conclusion

This study proposed the idea of utilizing segment information for each type of business in the formulation of business portfolio strategy, which is an element of corporate strategy. To this end, published data from Mitsubishi Electric Group was utilized. Thus, overall business evaluation of each business area (its strategic positioning in the group) was clarified using data on profitability (ROA and CFROA) and its relationship with consolidated performance, risk evaluation, growth, profitability variance analysis, approximated FCF analysis, inter-segment transactions, and inter-segment profitability correlation coefficients. Using these as a lead, segment information for each type of business based on the recent "management approach" can be considered to support formulation of business portfolio strategy at least in terms of the following:

(1) It becomes possible to conduct overall business evaluation that takes account not only of profitability and growth but also risk information and the relationship between business areas (contribution to other segments and the company as a whole).

(2) By using risk information (business β) to calculate RRR for each business area and calculating the variance between the resulting RRR (as a performance evaluation criterion) and the actual rate of return and analyzing the factors contributing to that variance, utilization of segment information as a strategic management control tool becomes possible.

References

Hiraoka, S. (2010). *A Study of Financial Metrics for Corporate and Business Valuation: Focusing on Economic Profit, Cash Flow, and Segment Information.* Japan: Soseisha Co., Ltd. (In Japanese.)

Hiraoka, S. (2014). Electrical equipment group's business segments/cash flow analysis, *The Review of Business Administration of Soka University*, Vol. 38, No. 2, pp. 139–148. (In Japanese.)

Hiraoka, S. (2016). Innovation strategies and segment reporting, in Hamada, K. and Hiraoka, S. (eds.), *Management of Innovation Strategy in Japanese Companies* (pp. 109–127). Singapore: World Scientific.

Hiraoka, S. (2017). Group strategy and segment information: Learning from the management approach and the Sony group, *Aoyama Accounting Review*, Vol. 7, pp. 41–48. (In Japanese.)

Hiraoka, S. (2019), Financial information analysis supporting business portfolio strategy: With reference to Mitsubishi Electric Group segment information, *Journal of Business Administration of Kwansei Gakuin University*, Vol. 60, No. 4 (Dr. Kazuki Hamada Commemoration edition, pp. 129–146. (First publication of this paper)). (In Japanese.)

Monden, Y. (1980), New developments in management organization and profit planning, *Accounting*, Vol. 4, pp. 26–36. (In Japanese.)

Monden, Y. and Fernand, W.F.H. (1995). Business portfolio strategy under risk, *JICPA Journal*, Vol.7, No. 5, pp. 20–30. (In Japanese.)

Rabino, S. and Wright, A. (1984). Applying financial portfolio and multiple criteria approaches to product line decisions, *Industrial Marketing Management*, Vol. 13, No. 14, pp. 233–240.

Solomons, D. (1968). Accounting and some proposed solutions, in Rappaport, Firmin, P.A. and Zeff. S.A. (eds.), *Public Reporting by Conglomerates. The Issues, the Problems, and Some Possible Solutions* (pp. 91–104). The proceedings of the symposium held at Tulane University in 1968.

Part 2

Management Controls for Various Industries and Organizations

Chapter 5

Management Control in Private Finance Initiative (PFI)/Public–Private Partnership (PPP)

Naoya Yamaguchi

*Graduate School of Professional Accountancy,
Aoyama Gakuin University, Tokyo 150-8366, Japan*

1. Introduction

Private finance initiative (PFI) is a public service provision scheme that utilizes the funds and know-how of the private sector, which was implemented initially in the United Kingdom (U.K.) in 1992. In Japan, it was introduced with the enforcement of the so-called PFI Law in 1999. Initially, the PFI Law only covered projects involving the development of new facilities. However, in recent years, the know-how of the private sector has been utilized in the operation and management of existing facilities by introducing the designated administrator (*Shitei Kanrisya*) and concession systems.

At present, various PFI/public–private partnership (PPP) methods are being implemented with the introduction of a scheme to reduce the financial burden by effectively utilizing public-owned spaces and integrating public services with profitable private businesses.

The following two points can be mentioned as features of PFI/PPP compared to other public service provision methods.

73

- Unlike the traditional public procurement (TPM), the provision of public services is comprehensively entrusted to private sector for the long term (i.e., long-term and comprehensive consignment).
- Unlike privatization, public sector still has the ultimate responsibility for the provision of public services (i.e., the public sector is responsible for providing public services).

Unlike privatization, PFI/PPP is a method of comprehensively entrusting the provision of public services to private sector. Therefore, although the main provider of public services is the private sector, the public sector still has the ultimate responsibility for the content, quantity, and quality of public services and the PFI/PPP business models. To succeed in PFI/PPP, it is important for the public sector to design a well-organized business model and control the business proposals and implementation strategies of private sector.

This paper explains the outline of PFI/PPP in Japan and discusses the management controls required in PFI/PPP for the public sector, especially the central government.

2. Definitions and Characteristics of PFI/PPP

HM Treasury in the U.K. defines PFI as follows (HM Stationary Office, 2000).

The public sector contracts to purchase quality services on a long-term basis so as to take advantage of private sector management skills incentivized by having private finance at risk.

Based on this definition, PFI has the following two characteristics, namely, *the use of private funds* and *provision of public services led by the private sector*.

Conversely, there are various definitions of PPP. For example, the International Monetary Fund (IMF) (2004) defines PPPs as *arrangements where the private sector supplies infrastructure assets and services that traditionally have been provided by the government*. However, this definition indicates disagreement on what constitutes a PPP. It describes that, in addition to private implementation and financing of public investment, PPPs have two other important characteristics, namely, an emphasis on service provision and investment by the private sector and transferring significant risk from the government to the private sector.

In addition, the Organization for Economic Co-operation and Development (OECD) (2008) defines a PPP as follows.

An agreement between the government and one or more private partners (which may include the operators and the financers) according to which the private partners deliver the service in such a manner that the service delivery objectives of the government are aligned with the profit objectives of the private partners and where the effectiveness of the alignment depends on a sufficient transfer of risk to the private partners.

Similar to the IMF definition (2004), this one indicates that there are currently no clear criteria for what constitutes a PPP. It clarifies that since PPPs occupy a middle ground between TPM and privatization, it is necessary to clearly distinguish between them with the distinguishing feature being whether sufficient risk has been transferred. In other words, the distinguishing feature between a PPP and privatization is the focus on partnership.

Additionally, it defines partnerships extensively as an extensive definition would include the cases where the partners share the same objectives and the cases where partners with different objectives are nevertheless able to align those objectives in such a manner that realizing the objectives of one party also implies the realization of the other party. In other words, if a PPP contract implies that the private partner will maximize its profit when delivering a service efficiently and effectively, then the contract constitutes a partnership since both parties (i.e., the government and the private partner) will achieve their objectives.

Moreover, it demonstrates that privatization involves no strict alignment of objectives, since the government is not usually involved in the output specification of the privatized entity, allowing the privatized entity to pursue maximum profit. However, in the case of PPP, the government usually details both the quantity and quality of the required service, and the government and the private partner agree upon the price when concluding the contract. The company would then expect its profit at the agreed price.

Based on the aforementioned definitions, PPPs have the following four characteristics.

- Long-term partnerships that align public sector interests with private sector interests.
- Provision of public services led by the private sector.
- Specification of public services by the public sector.
- Transfer of significant risks to the private sector.

3. Overview of PFI/PPP in Japan

To date, the Japanese PFI Law has been amended six times, contributing to the diversification of PFI/PPP schemes and the expansion of the business scope. They can be classified into the following five categories.

1. Establishment and expansion of the lending system for administrative property.
2. Expansion of the PFI target facilities.
3. Proposal systems by the private sector.
4. Introduction of the concession systems and its expansion of national support.
5. Financial support provided by the Private Finance Initiative Promotion Corporation of Japan (PFIPCJ).

By amending the PFI Law, in addition to the expansion of the scope of PFI/PPP businesses, the basic conditions for implementing PFI/PPP projects that utilize the private sector's know-how were established.

In 2013, the Committee for Promotion of PPP/PFI in the cabinet office decided upon the action plan for the radical reform of PPP/PFI, which presented the following four PFI/PPP types, establishing the scale target for each type and the specific initiative for its promotion.

1. PFI business utilizing the concession system (concession business).
2. PFI business collecting PFI expenses through other businesses' income such as the income from attached profitable facilities (profit type business).

3. PPP business utilizing private proposals such as the effective use of public real estate (public real estate utilization business).
4. Other types such as the deferred payment-type PFI business, performance-linked contracts, comprehensive contracts for multiple facilities, etc.

As a basic concept, the action plan aims at a fundamental shift from the deferred payment type. In particular, in addition to promoting the concession systems, the central government promotes the PFI businesses that enhance profitability by attaching and utilizing profitable facilities and collect PFI expenses using their incomes in addition to tax revenues. Moreover, for the broader PPPs, the central government promotes the businesses that boldly incorporate private proposals into the effective use of public real estate to realize the optimal services led by the private sector and maximize the values of local communities and the satisfaction of local residents.

In 2016, the committee decided upon the PPP/PFI promotion action plan, which indicated the importance of ingenuity such as enhancing the feasibility by *bundling* and *geographical broadening* for businesses that are small in scale and difficult to commercialize independently. The plan defines bundling as *a method for commercializing multiple facilities of the same type or different types in a lump,* and geographical broadening as *a method for implementing a single PPP/PFI business by multiple local governments as administrators of the public facility.*

According to a report published in 2017 by a subsection of Committee for Promotion of PPP/PFI, *Bundling* is classified into the following three forms:

- **Bundling by a single local government:** A method by which a single local government becomes an administrator of public facilities and commercializes these facilities in a lump.
- **Aggregation and compounding:** A method to consolidate and combine multiple facilities into a single facility.
- **Geographical broadening:** A method by which multiple local governments become administrators of public facilities and commercialize these facilities in a lump.

Thereby, in Japan, the revision of the PFI Law and the promotion of various business types and bundling/geographical broadening enabled designing a variety of PFI/PPP business models.

4. Difference between Public Management and Corporate Management

Lane (2009) argues for the difference thesis, claiming that politics and the public sector make for several differences between public and private management. He describes the objectives and setting as the characteristics of public management, pointing out the rule of law as the major restriction.

1. **Objectives:**
   a. Public management is the accomplishment of social objectives.
   b. Politics affects public management in a decisive manner when the basic goals of an organization are defined and determined.
   c. There is a distinction between provision and production in relation to public services, as it is not necessary to employ a public agency to deliver such services.
2. **Setting:**
   a. The setting of public management consists of politics, power, and the major public institutions of a country.
   b. The members of government have no ownership rights and no right to share the gains of the community.
3. **Many public services** are allocated outside the market, as it is difficult to reveal their value accurately. Thus, the value of public services tends to reflect the political preferences forthcoming in the democratic election process.
4. **Public services** are financed by taxes and regulated by the public law.
5. **Rule of law:**
   a. The elements of rule of law that restrain state management are numerous, and they constrain public management to an extent that has no correspondence in private management.

Lane (2009) indicates that the values of public services tend to reflect the political preferences, with the public services being regulated by the public law. Moreover, he indicates that it is necessary to fulfill the rule of law requirements. Given his argument, PFI/PPP implementation must also take into account the political process and the rule of law requirements.

5. Governance through Networks

Public management is often discussed using the concept of *Governance*. However, there is no clear definition of governance (Miyakawa, 2002; Nishioka, 2006; Uno, 2016).

Bevir (2012) demonstrates that *Governance* refers to all processes of governing; whether undertaken by a government, market, or network; whether over a family, tribe, formal or informal organization, or territory; and whether through laws, norms, power, or language. He indicates that although governance refers to the shift in public organizations since the 1980s, the word itself has a long history since the Middle Ages, and the concept of governance has waxed and waned in opposition to the belief in the sovereign state.

Additionally, he indicates that the crisis of the state destroyed faith in hierarchic bureaucracy in the 1970s and 1980s; therefore, policy-makers tried to reform the public sector by expanding market and network forms of organization, with the result being the rise of the new governance at the local, national, and global levels.

Rhodes (1996, 1997a, 1997b) presented the following six definitions of governance:

1. Governance as the minimal state.
2. Governance as corporate governance.
3. Governance as the new public management.
4. Governance as "good governance".
5. Governance as a socio-cybernetic system.
6. Governance as self-organizing networks.

Rhodes (2000) removed "governance as the minimal state" and added "governance as international interdependence," and "governance as the new political economy."

Rhodes (1996) defines governance as *self-organizing, inter-organizational networks*, listing its four shared characteristics as follows:

1. Interdependence between organizations. Governance is broader than government, covering non-state actors.
2. Continuing interactions between network members because of the need to exchange resources and negotiate shared objectives.
3. Game-like interactions, which are rooted in trust and regulated by the negotiated rules of the game agreed upon by network participants.
4. A significant degree of autonomy from the state. Networks are not accountable to the state, as they are self-organizing. However, although the state does not occupy a privileged, sovereign position, it can steer networks indirectly and imperfectly.

Bevir (2012) indicates that PPPs are in many ways just more formal versions of the networks that dominate public governance at present, with the rise of partnerships and networks placing a premium on the ability of public managers to steer them.

Moreover, he indicates that since one of the main characteristics of network governance is the relative absence of a single centralized authority, network managers have to consider that the networks contain interdependent actors, promote trust among these actors, manage conflicts among them, and maintain their commitment.

In consideration of Rhodes (1996) and Bevir (2012), since PFI/PPP is a form of *self-organizing network*, effective management of PFI/PPP networks is an important issue in their management control. Moreover, although the central government does not occupy a privileged, sovereign position in the networks, it can steer networks indirectly and imperfectly. Therefore, the central government has to support public agencies, which are directly responsible for the public services, so that they can promote trust with private partners, manage conflicts with them, and maintain their commitment.

6. Management Control in PFI/PPP Business

PFI/PPPs are schemes for the public and private partners to form a long-term partnership, with the private sector as the main provider leading the provision of the public services that the public sector defined as content, quantity, quality, and so forth. The key to success in PFI/PPP is the simultaneous realization of the social objectives through public services and the objectives of the private sector.

Thus, although the social objectives realized by PFI/PPPs include improving the quality of public services, increasing their quantity, preventing the reduction in their quantity, maintaining the stable supply (sustainability), reducing the cost, preventing the increase in cost, and so forth, it is decided upon through the political process which purposes are emphasized. If the social objectives realized through the PFI/PPP business are determined through the political process, public agencies must steer businesses to simultaneously realize the public and private interests.

When classifying the entities involving the PFI/PPP businesses into the following three actors, namely, the central government, the public agencies which are directly responsible for the public services (i.e., directly responsible entities), and private partners, it is extremely important to steer PFI/PPP business by the central government and directly responsible entities.

In the case of businesses under the direct control of the state, since the central government and the directly responsible entities are the same, the government can directly control the business. However, if local governments are directly responsible, the central government cannot directly control the businesses, so it is necessary to provide support for the success of the project, particularly, supporting the design of a business model that can achieve both the provision of high-quality public services that meet the needs of residents and the objectives of the private sector.

In Japan, the following five measures are implemented to support the PFI/PPP business models formulated by the central government.

1. Development of laws and regulations:
   a. Revision and enforcement of the PFI law.
   b. Enactment and revision of laws and regulations related to the business (e.g., Civil Park Law, Sewerage Law).
2. Development of guidelines:
   a. Process guidelines.
   b. Risk sharing guidelines.

    c. Value for Money (VFM) guidelines.

    d. Contract guidelines.

    e. Monitoring guidelines.

    f. Concession guidelines.

3. Creating manuals for simplified procedures:

    a. Manuals for simplified procedures of services provided to the public sector PFI business-type by local governments.

    b. PPP/PFI feasibility study simplified manuals (e.g., air conditioning maintenance and renewal of public facilities).

4. Horizontal development of information and technical know-how (regional block platforms):

    a. Market sounding.

    Local governments and private enterprises exchange opinions on the marketability and feasibility of the businesses under consideration by local governments.

    b. PPP/PFI promotion meetings by the heads of local governments.

    Mayors who want to promote community development through PFI/PPPs gather and exchange opinions on several issues.

    c. Training for local governments and private enterprises' employees to acquire practical knowledge of PFI/PPPs.

5. Support for individual local governments.

    a. Support projects for leading PPP businesses.

    (Ministry of Land, Infrastructure, Transport, and Tourism).

    Subsidies for the investigations required for the introduction of leading PPP businesses by local governments, and so forth.

    b. Support for designing PPP models.

    (Ministry of Land, Infrastructure, Transport, and Tourism).

    Dispatching consultants to small- and medium-sized local governments (municipalities with a population of approximately less than 200,000) to support the investigation and preparation of relevant materials necessary for implementing the following PFI/PPP businesses, namely, PPPs through collaboration of various fields, PPPs through geographical broadening, PPPs united with profitable private businesses, and other new PPP schemes that can be used in other regions.

    c. Support projects for investigation of businesses utilizing private finance (cabinet office).

Subsidies for investigation required for the introduction of concessions, and so forth.

d. Support for establishing regional platforms (cabinet office).

Support for establishing and operating debate forums to improve the ability to start PPP/PFI businesses in local regions, as the local governments, financial institutions, companies, etc., can gather to acquire the technical know-how and exchange information.

e. Support for establishing priority examination standards (cabinet office).

Dispatching the cabinet office staff and consultants to local governments to support the establishment of priority examination standards and investigate the implementation of PPP/PFI schemes according to these standards.

f. Support for private proposals system (cabinet office).

Support for a series of initiatives, such as public offering, reception, evaluation, and examination of the use for the PPP/PFI businesses, to introduce the ideas and capabilities of private enterprises by utilizing the proposal system by the private sector based on the PFI Law.

g. Support for launching new projects (cabinet office).

Support for starting new PPP/PFI businesses by clarifying the feasibility of the businesses and presenting future directions at the examination stage.

h. Support for problem examination by advanced experts (cabinet office).

Dispatching advanced experts in law, accounting, tax, finance, and so forth, to the local governments, which are considering implementing concession businesses, profit-based businesses, and public real estate utilization projects that require advanced professional examination, for advising and providing information.

7. Conclusion

PFI/PPPs are schemes for the public and private sectors to form a long-term partnership, with the private sector, as the main provider, leading the provision of the public services that the public sector defined as content, quantity, quality, and so forth.

The key to success in PFI/PPP is the simultaneous realization of the social objectives through public services and the objectives of the private sector. In Japan, the revision of the PFI Law and the promotion of various business types and bundling/geographical broadening have enabled the designing of a business model that would allow the reduction or the prevention of an increase in the public financial burden and the profit acquisition of the private sector.

However, as Lane (2009) points out, politics plays a crucial role in the decision-making process in the public sector, which is also true for PFI/PPP businesses such as regarding the utilization of PFI/PPP schemes, and the selection of business models when assumed to be utilized.

If local governments are directly responsible for the PFI/PPP businesses, the central government cannot directly control them because local governments make decisions for them autonomously through their own political processes.

Therefore, the central government's approach to manage and control the PFI/PPP businesses should focus on supporting the local governments in designing PFI/PPP business models, so that they can promote trust with private partners, manage conflicts with them, and maintain their commitment.

In this regard, in Japan, the central government has implemented various support measures such as adopting laws, regulations, guidelines, and manuals for simplifying procedures, the horizontal development of information and technical know-how, and support for individual local governments. Through these support measures, the number of PFI/PPP businesses has been steadily increasing, with the number of local governments introducing PFI/PPP schemes increasing as well. However, there are many local governments, which are mainly small- and medium-sized, that have no PFI/PPP schemes or with little utilization.

In Japan, the environment surrounding public services has been deteriorating, with huge public debts, decreases in tax and usage fee revenues due to the population decline and the widening of regional disparities regarding these decreases, and the deterioration of public facilities. To ensure the sustainability of public services in a society in the midst of full-fledged population decline, it is essential to actively utilize the PFI/PPP schemes in most local governments.

Further, although the issue of how public agencies control the private enterprises' business proposals and implementation is pointed out as another point of the argument for PFI/PPP management control, it would be discussed at another opportunity.

References

Bevir, M. (2012). *Governance: A Very Short Introduction*. Oxford: Oxford University Press.

HM Stationary Office, (2000). *Public Private Partnerships — The Government's Approach*.

International Monetary Fund, Fiscal Affairs Department, (2004). *Public-Private Partnerships*.

Lane, J.E. (2009). *State Management: An Enquiry into Models of Public Administration and Management*. Abingdon: Routledge.

Miyakawa, T. (2002). 1-1 What's governance?, in Miyakawa, T. and K. Yamamoto (eds.), *Public Governance — Reform and Strategy, Nihon Keizai Hyouronsya*. (In Japanese.)

Nishioka, S. (2006). Genealogy of public governance theories, in Iwasaki, M. and N. Tanaka (eds.), *Governance in the Public and Private Domains*. Kanagawa: Tokai University Press Office. (In Japanese.)

Organization for Economic Co-operation and Development (OECD), (2008). *Public-Private Partnerships: In Pursuit of Risk Sharing and Value for Money*.

Rhodes, R.A.W. (1996). The new governance: Governing without government, *Political Studies*, Vol. XLIV, pp. 652–667.

Rhodes, R.A.W. (1997a). *Understanding Governance: Policy Networks, Governance, Reflexivity and Accountability*. Maidenhead: Open University Press.

Rhodes, R.A.W. (1997b). Foreword: Governance and networks, in Stoker, G. (ed.), *The New Management of British Local Governance*. Hampshire: Macmillan Press Ltd.

Rhodes, R.A.W. (2000), Governance and public administration, in Pierre, J. (ed.), *Debating Governance*, Chapter 4. Oxford: Oxford University Press.

Uno, S. (2016), Governance in history of political thoughts, In M. Osawa, and I. Sato (eds.), *Reviewing Governance I: The Future of Cross-Border Theory of Governance*, Chapter 1. Institute of Social Science, University of Tokyo, Tokyo. (In Japanese.)

Chapter 6

Impact of Co-Developing Performance Measures with Employees on Organization Performance: A Survey of Local Governments in Japan

Takehiro Metoki

Faculty of Economics, Musashi University,
Tokyo 176-8534, Japan

1. Introduction

The purpose of this study is to clarify the relationship between operational employee involvement patterns, environmental factors, and organizational performance in the design and use of performance measures in a performance management system (PMS). The issue of how operational employees should participate in the design and use of management accounting systems to enhance their effects is one of the important themes in recent management accounting research (De Baerdemaeker and Bruggeman, 2015; Derfuss, 2009; Kruis and Widener, 2014; Luft and Shields, 2007). Since operational employees have specialized knowledge of tasks compared to senior managers (Kim *et al.*, 2014), the quality of performance indicators is improved by involving them in the process of designing and using performance measures. In addition, some empirical evidence also shows the improvement in organizational performance (Groen *et al.*, 2012, 2016; Hunton and Gibson, 1999; Kleingeld *et al.*,

2004). It has also been observed that the involvement of operational employees affects the acceptance and rejection of performance information, not only in companies but also in public sector (Petersen *et al.*, 2019). Conversely, it is understood that the involvement of operational employees in the management accounting system does not necessarily have a positive effect (De Baerdemaeker and Bruggeman, 2015; Kruis and Widener, 2014). For example, in traditional budgeting, participation of operational employees in setting budget targets increases their motivation, while resulting in budget slack that under reports the target level. It is also known to reduce the budget effect. In this way, the involvement of operational employees in the design and use of management accounting systems has a positive effect, but attention must be paid to the possibility of negative effects.

Therefore, how and to what extent should operational employees be involved in the design and use of performance measures in a PMS? Groen *et al.* (2017) analyzed the relationship between operational employee involvement and job performance, focusing on the design and use of performance measures that affect the effectiveness of the PMS. Their results clarified that the involvement of operational employees does not necessarily improve performance, but the effect on performance depends on the purpose of using performance measures. Poon *et al.* (2001) pointed out that the involvement of operational employees wastes time for adjustment, resulting in disagreements and conflicts. Excessive participation of operational employees in performance measurement related process may hinder their performance, resulting in performance degradation.

Previous studies assume that the greater the involvement of operational employees in the design and use of performance measures, the more positive the performance. However, so far, there has not been enough consideration on the following question: to what extent should an operational employee be involved, and in which process, regarding the design and use of performance measures? Furthermore, it is not clear how operational employees should be involved in PMS in the context of administrative organizations. In this study, we analyze the relationship between operational employee involvement patterns, environmental factors, and organizational performance in the design and use of performance indicators in PMS, using questionnaire survey data.

2. Previous Research and Analytical Framework

2.1 *Involvement of operational employees in the design and use of performance measures in a PMS*

In general, the involvement of operational employees in system design increases user satisfaction and reduces user cognitive dissonance (Wouters and Wilderom, 2008). As for PMS, it has been shown that the involvement of operational employees in performance measure design improves the quality of performance indicators, suppresses measurement errors, and has a positive effect on the organization (Abernethy and Bouwens, 2005). Operational employees have more specialized knowledge and information about their tasks than managers, and can improve the quality of performance measures by reflecting them in performance measures (Wouters and Roijmans, 2011). It has been shown that the involvement of operational employees, directly or indirectly, has a positive impact on the performance of individuals and organizations (Groen *et al.*, 2012, 2016; Hunton and Gibson, 1999; Kleingeld *et al.*, 2004). Groen *et al.* (2012) analyzed the process by which operational employees design performance measures related to their work, targeting the bottling line in the beverage manufacturing industry. Consequently, they clarified that the involvement of operational employees in the process of designing the performance measures of their departments will improve their willingness to work and will initiate improvement in the performance of their departments. Thus, it has been clarified that the involvement of operational employees in the design and use of performance measures in a PMS not only enhances the individual attitude toward work but also improves organizational performance. Conversely, it has also been pointed out that the involvement of operational employees in the design and use of performance measures does not necessarily have a positive effect. Kruis and Widener (2014) reveal that some managers are critical of involving operational employees in the process of designing and using performance measures. In other words, the involvement of operational employees wastes time in opinion adjustment and can lead to disagreements and conflicts within the organization (Poon *et al.*, 2001). Groen *et al.* (2017) clarified that the involvement of operational employees does not necessarily improve performance. They analyzed the relationship between operational employee involvement and job performance using data from a questionnaire survey conducted on both managers and their operational employees. Their results showed that the involvement of operational employees enhances their job performance only when performance measures are used to assess the performance of their department. But when performance measures were used to determine monetary and non-monetary rewards, the involvement of operational employees had no impact on their job performance. Thus, the main claim of previous studies is that the involvement of operational employees in the design and usage process of performance measures increases performance. However, recent studies have shown that the involvement of operational employees does not necessarily give positive results.

2.2 *The design and use of performance measures*

Research on operational employees in a PMS has considered their involvement as a series of processes. In practice, however, the involvement of operational employees consists of multiple processes. This is divided into five stages: (1) design of performance measures, (2) selection of data used as input for performance measures, (3) modification of performance measures, (4) implementation of performance measures, and (5) maintenance of performance measures (Bourne *et al.*, 2000; Groen *et al.*, 2017; Neely *et al.*, 2002). For example, the questionnaire survey in Groen *et al.* (2017) also asks the degree of participation in the above five processes in order to measure the degree of involvement in the process related to performance indicators. However, the five question items are combined into one factor in the analysis. Therefore, little consideration has been given to the extent to which the operational employee should be involved in each process, and what kind of involvement pattern will enhance performance.

2.3 *Classification of management accounting systems (configuration research)*

Management accounting system is not uniform and has various features, depending on its design and use. Therefore, many studies in recent management accounting research aim at the construction of stricter management accounting theory by typifying the characteristics of management accounting system. For example, Sponem and Lambert (2016) categorized the characteristics of the budget management system using cluster analysis with 11 variables, and analyzed the relationship between each cluster and budget satisfaction. Similarly, Kruis *et al.* (2016) performed cluster analysis and typified combinations that balanced the four control concepts in Simons' (1994) LOC framework, which consisted of belief control, boundary control, diagnostic control, and interactive control. In this way, clustering the management accounting system enables more precise analysis.

3. Research Frameworks

3.1 *Research methods*

In order to categorize the involvement pattern of operational employees in design and use of performance measures in a PMS, this study performs a cluster analysis that inputs the evolution process into performance measures as a variable. Kruis *et al.* (2016) believe that an organization's environmental factors also affect the classification, and therefore, they are also included in the cluster analysis. Following this, we also consider the relationship between each cluster and the environmental factors. In addition, in order to clarify whether there is a difference in organizational performance between clusters, variance analysis and multiple comparisons are performed on the relationship between each cluster and organizational performance.

3.2 *Data*

Data for analysis was collected by mailing a questionnaire survey; the survey was conducted in FY2016 in 791 Japanese cities (designated cities, core cities, special cities, and other cities). Prior to sending the questionnaire, we asked two practitioners who supervised the related work in the administrative organization, and two management accounting researchers with specialized knowledge in performance management, to check the validity of the wordings and question items. The questionnaire was received by the management department supervisor of the administrative

Table 1.   Response distribution.

Group classification	Number of surveys sent	Number of valid responses (Rate)	
Designated cities	20	14	70.0%
Core cities	48	20	41.7%
Special cities	36	8	22.2%
Other cities	687	285	41.5%
Total	791	327	41.3%

organization, and it was sent with a request letter and reply envelope. In consideration of incentives for answering the questionnaire, it was clarified that a report on the analysis results will be sent to the respondent. In order to improve the collection rate, a reminder was sent before the response deadline. The final number of responding organizations was 339 (recovery rate 42.9%). The collected data excluded those organizations that gave inadequate responses and were judged inappropriate for analysis. The number of valid responses was 327 (valid response rate 41.3%). Details of the responding organizations are shown in Table 1. Additionally, respondents comprised staff at a section manager level or higher in the concerned department. A goodness-of-fit test was performed on the data collected from 327 administrative organizations used in the analysis. The results confirmed that the data were generally compatible with the group distribution ($\chi^2 = 7.770$, $df = 3$, $p = 0.051$). Additionally, we conducted a test of the difference between the size of the target organization and the non-target organization (administrative organization: number of employees), but no significant difference was found between the two. The results did not show any significant non-response bias in the data.

4. Variable Manipulation

4.1 *Involvement of operational employees in the design and use of performance measures*

Based on Bourne *et al.* (2000), this study discusses the involvement of organizational members in the design and use of management systems. Moreover, the study sets and amends performance measures, collects data,

Table 2. The involvement in process of design and use of performance measure.

Items	Range	Mean	S. D.
Design of performance measures	1–5	3.72	0.801
Selection of data used as input for performance	1–5	3.63	0.829
Implementation of performance measures	1–5	3.60	0.822
Modification of performance measures	1–5	3.88	0.713
Maintenance of performance measures	1–5	3.65	0.821

and conducts analysis to achieve numerical targets for performance measures. Five questions are set regarding the degree of participation of non-managerial staff in processes such as the evaluation of the achievement status of the performance measures (Table 2). The responses to the above questions were based on a 5-point scale, ranging from "1 (not participating at all)" to "5 (actively participating)."

4.2 *Environmental factors*

In order to control the analysis results, the number of employees was set as a control variable; this is because items such as environmental uncertainty, business complexity, and organization scale are expected to affect the performance management of administrative organizations. Regarding environmental uncertainties and operational complexity, we referred to Speklé and Verbeeten (2014) and Oura and Matsuo (2017) to set questions and conduct exploratory factor analysis (main factor method and Promax rotation). Additionally, when conducting factor analysis, items for which the ceiling effect was confirmed and items that showed only factor loadings below 0.4 for all factors were deleted. Consequently, the first factor denoting the environmental uncertainty had a high factor loading in the item indicating uncertainties related to the future predictability of work, and therefore this factor was termed "Task predictability" ($\alpha = 0.778$). The second factor was named "Business design difficulty" ($\alpha = 0.692$) because it showed a high factor loading in the items indicating difficulty in predicting needs and effects related to business design (upper part of Table 3). Although Cronbach's α of "business predictability," which is the first factor, is below the general standard of 0.70, there is no major problem in reliability

Table 3.   Factor analysis on the control variables.

Uncertainty of the task environment	Range	Mean	S.D.	Factor 1 Task predictability ($\alpha = 0.778$)	Factor 2 Business design difficulty ($\alpha = 0.692$)
When designing a business, it is difficult to predict needs	1–5	2.72	0.739	0.807	−0.061
When designing a business, it is difficult to predict the effect	1–5	2.84	0.804	0.792	0.060
There is a high possibility that unpredictable events will occur in daily operations	1–5	3.11	0.888	−0.057	0.735
It is difficult to predict when a new project will start	1–5	3.11	0.965	0.055	0.724
Eigenvalue				1.869	1.310
Factor correlation			Factor 1	—	
			Factor 2	0.238	—

Business complexity	Range	Mean	S.D.	Factor 1 Business process clarity ($\alpha = 0.792$)	Factor 2 Measurable outcome ($\alpha = 0.777$)
There is an appropriate and efficient process for conducting business	1–5	3.02	0.933	**0.804**	−0.002
There is a standard procedure that should be referenced for addressing differences in business execution	1–5	2.93	1.071	**0.779**	−0.037
Business execution procedures are clearly shared among various departments	1–5	3.26	0.904	**0.674**	0.067

Table 3. *(Continued)*

Business complexity	Range	Mean	S.D.	Factor 1 Business process clarity ($\alpha = 0.792$)	Factor 2 Measurable outcome ($\alpha = 0.777$)
Procedures for conducting business are stipulated through laws, regulations, and rules, among others	1–5	3.21	0.983	**0.539**	−0.012
A single quantitative measure can grasp the results of each business	1–5	2.51	0.963	−0.051	**0.847**
Quantitatively understand what the department should achieve	1–5	2.87	0.939	0.061	**0.749**
Eigenvalue				2.867	1.255
Factor correlation				Factor 1	—
				Factor 2	0.424	—

because it is judged to be close to 0.70. The first factor of business complexity is "Business process clarity" ($\alpha = 0.792$) because it had a high factor loading in the item indicating whether business procedures and processes were clarified by manuals and regulations. The second factor was named "Measurable outcome" ($\alpha = 0.777$) because it showed a high factor loading on the items related to the measurable outcome of the department (lower part of Table 3). Additionally, in the variabilization of each item, the average value of the question items that showed a factor load of 0.4 or more was scored. Finally, in order to control the scale of the organization, the value obtained through logarithmic conversion of the number of employees was used in the analysis. In addition, average variance extracted (AVE) was calculated to determine the discriminative validity of factors related to environmental uncertainties and operational complexity, but both factors exceeded 0.5 and were discriminative. There was no problem with validity.

4.3 *Organizational performance*

The use of PMS brings various benefits to an organization. Non-financial as well as financial results have been used for performance assessment, as shown in many quantitative studies (e.g., Davis and Albright, 2004; Ittner and Larcker, 2001). However, administrative organizations cannot measure performance using financial results, such as sales and profit measures. Therefore, many public sector studies have relied on the items from Van de Ven and Ferry (1980), which are considered suitable for measuring public sector performance. Measurements were made using the following seven items: quantity or amount of work produced; quality or accuracy of work produced; number of innovations or new ideas by the unit; reputation of "work excellence"; attainment of unit production or service goals; efficiency of unit operations; and morale of unit personnel. I have developed a set of measurements based on Van de Ven and Ferry's measurements, but with some modifications. In this study, we added six items, such as budget adjustment and cost awareness, which were measured by major PMS studies, such as Hall (2008). We conducted an exploratory factor analysis (using the main factor method and Promax rotation) on the performance of administrative organizations, based on these 13 questions. We identified the elements that contribute to the performance of administrative organizations. Consequently, as shown in Table 4, it became clear that the performance of administrative organizations is composed of two

Table 4.   Factor analysis on the performance of administrative organizations.

Items	Range	Mean	S.D.	Factor 1 Behavioral performance ($\alpha = 0.795$)	Factor 2 Task performance ($\alpha = 0.733$)
Adjustment of budgets and plans in other departments	1–5	3.26	0.825	**0.765**	−0.103
Information exchange with staff in other departments	1–5	3.18	0.763	**0.665**	−0.029
Improvement in cost reduction awareness	1–5	3.38	0.762	**0.662**	0.085

Table 4.   *(Continued)*

Items	Range	Mean	S.D.	Factor 1 Behavioral performance ($\alpha = 0.795$)	Factor 2 Task performance ($\alpha = 0.733$)
Reduction in the time incurred for making decision associated with goals, policies, and work schedule	1–5	3.02	0.734	**0.572**	0.038
Improvement staff motivation toward work	1–5	3.19	0.699	**0.534**	0.185
Quality or accuracy of work	1–5	3.43	0.668	–0.142	**0.931**
Increase in business volume (production volume) and service provision	1–5	3.18	0.677	0.095	**0.513**
Improvement in the achievement of business and departmental goals	1–5	3.67	0.665	0.241	**0.501**
Eigenvalue				3.601	1.113
Factor correlation			Factor 1	—	—
			Factor 2	0.586	—

factors. The first factor is named "Behavioral performance" because items related to the impact on staff behavior, such as cost awareness and motivation, showed a high factor loading ($\alpha = 0.795$). The second factor was named "Task performance" because it comprised the result of work activities, such as work quality, efficiency, and achievement of departmental goals ($\alpha = 0.733$). In addition, when calculating the AVE of both factors related to the organizational performance, Cronbach's α exceeded the general standard of 0.7, although it was slightly below 0.5; therefore, we decided to use it for this analysis.

Cluster analysis was performed using these measures. The basic statistics for the measurement scale are shown in Table 5, and the correlation coefficient between variables is shown in Table 6.

Table 5.　Descriptive statistics.

Variables	Number of items	Min.	Max.	Mean	S.D.	Cronbach Alpha	AVE
Design of performance measures	1	1.00	5.00	3.72	0.801	N/A	N/A
Selection of data used as input for performance measures	1	1.00	5.00	3.63	0.829	N/A	N/A
Implementation of performance measures	1	1.00	5.00	3.60	0.822	N/A	N/A
Modification of performance measures	1	1.00	5.00	3.88	0.713	N/A	N/A
Maintenance of performance measures	1	1.00	5.00	3.65	0.821	N/A	N/A
Business design difficulty	2	1.00	5.00	2.78	0.698	0.778	0.639
Task predictability	2	1.50	5.00	3.11	0.810	0.692	0.532
Business process clarity	4	1.00	5.00	2.98	0.910	0.792	0.500
Measurable outcome	2	1.25	4.75	2.97	0.668	0.777	0.639
Behavioral performance	5	1.40	5.00	3.21	0.561	0.795	0.416
Task performance	3	1.00	5.00	3.41	0.555	0.733	0.460

5.　Results

The purpose of this study is to clarify the involvement pattern of operational employees in the design and use of performance indicators in a PMS. Therefore, we conducted a hierarchical cluster analysis with variables for each process related to the involvement of operational employees. In the analysis, input variables are standardized. In order to interpret each cluster, one-way variance analysis was performed, and then multiple comparisons were performed using the Tukey method (Table 7). Three clusters were determined based on the dendrogram created as a result of analysis based on the Ward method.

Cluster 1 was named "Data Selection and Implementation Type" because the involvement of operational employees in data selection and implementation was relatively high than in other processes. Although the

Table 6. Correlation coefficient between variables.

Variables	(1)	(2)	(3)	(4)	(5)	(6)	(7)	(8)	(9)	(10)	(11)
Design of performance measures	1										
Selection of data used as input for performance measures	0.699**	1									
Implementation of performance measures	0.745**	0.723**	1								
Modification of performance measures	0.640**	0.599**	0.630**	1							
Maintenance of performance measures	0.618**	0.607**	0.626**	0.720**	1						
Business design difficulty	−0.051	−0.144**	−0.083**	−0.102	−0.101	1					
Task predictability	−0.070	−0.013	−0.026**	−0.030	0.001	0.179**	1				
Business process clarity	0.079	0.087	0.130	0.174**	0.121*	−0.163**	−0.247*	1			
Measurable outcome	0.069	0.098	0.113	0.156*	0.186**	−0.196**	−0.145*	0.557**	1		
Behavioral performance	0.281**	0.298**	0.309**	0.301	0.289**	−0.139*	0.018	−0.213***	0.282**	1	
Task performance	0.371**	0.353**	0.322**	0.364	0.266**	−0.141**	−0.051	−0.137*	0.231**	0.519**	1

Note: (1) Pearson's correlation coefficient.
(2) **$p < 0.01$, *$p < 0.05$ (two-tailed).

Table 7.   Multiple comparisons between clusters.

	Cluster 1 ($n = 149$)	Cluster 2 ($n = 148$)	Cluster 3 ($n = 26$)	ANOVA F-value	ANOVA p-value	Multiple comparison Tukey method
Design of performance measures	3.29	4.23	2.15	216.224	0.000	C2 > C1 > C3
Selection of data used as input for performance measures	3.53	4.22	2.04	202.412	0.000	C2 > C1 > C3
Implementation of performance measures	3.29	4.20	2.00	254.701	0.000	C2 > C1 > C3
Modification of performance measures	3.66	4.29	2.85	92.958	0.000	C2 > C1 > C3
Maintenance of performance measures	3.28	4.24	2.42	168.568	0.000	C2 > C1 > C3
Business design difficulty	2.84	2.70	2.85	1.567	0.210	—
Task predictability	3.14	3.06	3.25	0.722	0.486	—
Business process clarity	2.87	3.13	2.81	3.520	0.031	C2 > C1, C3
Measurable outcome	2.88	3.07	2.90	3.255	0.040	C2 > C1, C3
Behavioral performance	3.11	3.35	2.83	12.777	0.000	C2 > C1, C3
Task performance	3.34	3.56	2.97	15.989	0.000	C2 > C1> C3

cluster was moderately involved in all processes, the average value was higher in the implementation for selecting the data used as performance measures and achieving the goals for performance measures. Cluster 2 was named "All Process Type" because it was highly involved in all processes. Finally, although the degree of participation in Cluster 3 was low, only the involvement of operational employees in the implementation of performance measures was relatively higher than other processes; therefore, it was named "Implementation type." The ratio of each cluster was: 46% for Cluster 1 ("Data Selection and Implementation Type"), 46% for Cluster 2 ("All Process Type"), and 8% for Cluster 3 ("Implementation type"). In addition, the difference in the scale was confirmed using the value obtained by logarithmic conversion of the number of staff as the proxy variable in the scale, but no significant difference was confirmed. There were no significant differences between the clusters in terms of environmental uncertainty. In terms of performance, both behavioral performance and task performance were highest in Cluster 2 when compared to other clusters.

6. Conclusion

Three clusters were identified as patterns of involvement in processes related to performance measures of operational employees from the cluster analysis results. Previous studies measured the degree of involvement of operational employees in the design and use of performance measures as a series of processes. Therefore, the relationship between the pattern of employee involvement and organizational performance was not necessarily clarified. Therefore, it was not clear which process needs to be involved in order to achieve higher performance when operational employees are involved in each performance measure process. Through this study, the involvement pattern of field employees was clarified. The first is the "all process type," in which field employees are actively involved in all five stages of the process, from design to maintenance of performance. The second is the "data selection and implementation type," which is highly involved in the selection of data for performance measures and the implementation of goals related to performance measures. The third is the "implementation type" that involves only the performance of goals related to performance measures. The above three types were confirmed. Regarding the relationship between each type of involvement and organizational performance, the following became clear. Both "behavioral performance," composed of items such as cost awareness and motivation, and "task performance," composed of items representing the results of business activities such as improvement of work quality, efficiency, and residents' satisfaction, are higher in "all process types," where field employees are actively involved in all five stages of the process compared to other types. Instead of involving operational employees only in specific processes, it is suggested that active involvement of operational employees in all processes related to performance measures may improve organizational performance. This result is consistent with studies of Abernethy and Bouwens (2005), Wouters and Roijmans (2011), and Groen *et al.* (2012), where the involvement of operational employees increased organizational and individual performance. In addition, the degree of involvement of operational employees may be related to whether the business process is clear or whether it is easy to measure outcomes quantitatively. In business operations where the business process is complex or the work procedures are not manualized, it may be difficult for the operational employees to be involved. Therefore, by simplifying business processes and removing task complexity, such as by dividing tasks, field employees can be actively involved in performance indicators, leading to improved organizational performance.

References

Abernethy, M.A. and Bouwens, J. (2005). Determinants of accounting innovation implementation, *Abacus*, Vol. 41, No. 3, pp. 217–240.

Bourne, M., Mills, J. *et al.* (2000). Designing, implementing and updating performance measurement systems, *International Journal of Operation and Production Management*, Vol. 20, No. 7, pp. 754–771.

Davis, S. and Albright, T. (2004). An investigation of the effect of balanced scorecard implementation on financial performance, *Management Accounting Research*, Vol. 15, No. 2, pp. 135–153.

De Baerdemaeker, J. and Bruggeman, W. (2015). The impact of participation in strategic planning on managers' creation of budgetary slack: The mediating role of autonomous motivation and affective organizational commitment, *Management Accounting Research*, Vol. 29, pp. 1–12.

Derfuss, K. (2009). The relationship of budgetary participation and reliance on accounting performance measures with individual-level consequent variables: A meta-analysis, *European Accounting Review*, Vol. 18, pp. 203–239.

Groen, B.A.C., Wouters, M.J.F. *et al.* (2012). Why do employees take more initiative if they develop their own performance measures? A field study, *Management Accounting Research*, Vol. 23, No. 2, pp. 120–141.

Groen, B.A.C., Wilderom, C.P.M. *et al.* (2016). High job performance through co-developing performance measures with employees, *Human Resource Management*, Vol. 56, No. 1, pp. 111–132.

Groen, B.A.C., Wouters, M.J.F. *et al.* (2017). Employee participation, performance metrics, and job performance: A survey study based on self-determination theory, *Management Accounting Research*, Vol. 36, pp. 51–66.

Hall, M. (2008). The effect of comprehensive performance measurement systems on role clarity, psychological empowerment and managerial performance, *Accounting, Organizations and Society*, Vol. 33, No. 2/3, pp. 141–163.

Hunton, J.E. and Gibson, D. (1999). Soliciting user-input during the development of an accounting information system: Investigating the efficacy of group discussion, *Accounting, Organizations and Society*, Vol. 24, pp. 597–618.

Ittner, C.D. and Larcker, D.F. (2001). Assessing empirical research in management accounting: A value-based perspective, *Journal of Accounting and Economics*, Vol. 32, pp. 349–410.

Kim, Y.H., Sting, F.J. *et al.* (2014). Top-down, bottom-up, or both? Toward an integrative perspective on operations strategy formation, *Journal of Operation Management*, Vol. 32, No. 7–8, pp. 462–474.

Kleingeld, A., Van Tuijl, H. *et al.* (2004). Participation in the design of performance management systems: A quasiexperimental field study, *Journal of Organization Behaviour*, Vol. 25, pp. 831–851.

Kruis, A.M. and Widener, S.K. (2014). Managerial influence in performance measurement system design: A recipe for failure?, *Behavioral Research in Accounting*, Vol. 26, No. 2, pp. 1–34.

Kruis, A.M., Speklé, R.F. *et al.* (2016). The levers of control framework: An exploratory analysis of balance, *Management Accounting Research*, Vol. 32, pp. 27–44.

Luft, J.L. and Shields, M.D. (2007). Mapping management accounting: Graphics and guidelines for theory-consistent empirical research, in Chapman, C.S., Hopwood, A.G. *et al.* (eds.), *Handbook of Management Accounting Research* (Vol. 1), (pp. 27–98). Oxford, UK: Elsevier.

Neely, A.D., Bourne, M. *et al.* (2002). *Getting the Measure of Your Business*. Cambridge: University Press.

Oura, K. and Matsuo, T. (2017). The use of performance management information and its effectiveness in Japanese local government, *Journal of Cost Accounting in Japan*, Vol. 41, No. 1, pp. 103–115. (In Japanese.)

Petersen, N.B.G., Laumann, T. *et al.* (2019). Acceptance or disapproval: Performance information in the eyes of public frontline employees, *Journal of Public Administration Research And Theory*, Vol. 29, No.1, pp.101–117.

Poon, M., Pike, R. *et al.* (2001). Budget participation, goal interdependence and controversy: A study of a Chinese public utility, *Management Accounting Research*, Vol. 12, pp. 101–118.

Simons, R. (1994). How new top managers use control systems as levers of strategic renewal, *Strategic Management Journal*, Vol. 15, pp. 169–189.

Speklé, R.F. and Verbeeten, F.H.M. (2014). The use of performance measurement systems in the public sector: Effects on performance, *Management Accounting Research*, Vol. 25, No. 2, pp. 131–146.

Sponem, S. and Lambert, C. (2016). Exploring differences in budget characteristics, roles and satisfaction: A configurational approach, *Management Accounting Research*, Vol. 30, pp. 47–61.

Van de Ven, A.H. and Ferry, D.L. (1980). *Measuring and Assessing Organizations*. New York: Wiley.

Wouters, M.J.F. and Roijmans, D. (2011). Using prototypes to induce experimentation and knowledge integration in the development of enabling accounting information, *Contemporary Accounting Research*, Vol. 28, No. 2, pp. 708–736.

Wouters, M.J.F. and Wilderom, C.P.M. (2008). Developing performance-measurement systems as enabling formalization: A longitudinal field study of a logistics department, *Accounting, Organizations and Society*, Vol. 33, No. 4/5, pp. 488–516.

Chapter 7

The Impact and Effect of Management Control Systems on the Productivity of the Lodging Industry in Japan

Tsutomu Yoshioka

Faculty of International Tourism Management, Toyo University,
Tokyo 112-8606, Japan

1. Introduction

Unfortunately, it is well known that the productivity of the service industry in Japan, especially the lodging industry, is quite low. For example, labor productivity in 36 countries in OECD, The Organisation for Economic Co-operation and Development, is in the 20th position. In addition, the position of labor productivity per hour is the 21st (see Table 1). Moreover, it is the lowest in each of the seven major advanced (developed) countries (see Table 2). Also, the average value added per employee in the lodging industry is lower than the average for all industries in Japan (see Fig. 1).

Will the management control systems (MCS) of this industry play a role in building a productive system for companies in these industries? In addition, how effective is MCS and how does it affect the productivity of these service industries?

This paper clarifies these problems using literature reviews, interviews with industry workers, and examples as case studies.

Table 1. Ranking of labor productivity.

	Labor productivity per labor		Labor productivity per labor hour	
Ranking	Country	(US$)	Country	(US$)
1	Ireland	164,795	Ireland	97.5
2	Luxembourg	143,770	Luxembourg	94.7
3	United States	127,075	Norway	82.3
4	Norway	122,902	Belgium	73.5
5	Switzerland	118,155	Denmark	72.2
:	:	:	:	:
20	:	:	**Japan**	**47.5**
21	**Japan**	**84,027**	:	:
Average		95,464		53.5

Source: Japan Productivity Center (2018).

Table 2. Labor productivity of seven advanced (or developed) countries in OECD.

	Labor productivity per labor		Labor productivity per labor hour	
Ranking	Country	(US$)	Country	(US$)
1	United States	127,075	United States	72.0
2	France	106,998	Germany	69.8
3	Italy	104,179	France	67.8
4	Germany	100,940	Italy	55.5
5	Canada	93,093	Canada	53.7
6	United Kingdom	89,674	United Kingdom	53.5
7	**Japan**	**84,027**	**Japan**	**47.5**

Source: Japan Productivity Center (2018).

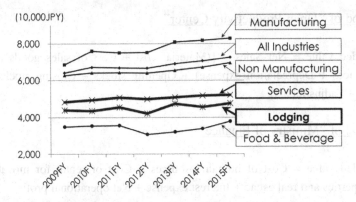

Fig. 1.   Labor productivity by industries in Japan.

Source: Policy Research Institute, Ministry of Finance, Japan (2015).

2. Literature Reviews

2.1 *Productivity*

Stewart and Johns (1996) say "Productivity may broadly be defined as the ratio of output to input". And productivity is generally calculated with the following formula:

$$\text{Productivity} = \frac{\text{Output}}{\text{Input}}$$

Generally, in Management Accounting research, labor productivity is calculated by substituting the added value generated by the company for Output and the number of employees or total working hours of the company for Input.

Several calculation methods are shown for the Added Value to be substituted for Output. Kajiura (2016) and Mizuno (2019) introduce these calculation methods as follows:

<u>Method of "Bank of Japan"</u>

Added value = Labor costs + Cost of rental + Net financial cost + Operational profit after taxes + Taxes + Depreciation expense

Method of "Japan Productivity Center"

Added value = Net Sales − {(Material cost + Cost of sales goods and services + Depreciation expense) + Opening stocks − Closing stocks + (or −) adjustments}

Method of "Ministry of Finance"

Added value = Cost of human resources + Cost of rental for movable properties and real estate + Interest expense + Net operational profit

(Operational profit − interest expense) + Taxes

What is common in both formulas is that the value generated by the company, the Added Value, is calculated.

2.2 *Management control system*

There are many previous researches on MCS. In this paper, Aoki (2015) is taken. This is because Aoki (2015) deals with MCS research focusing on interpersonal service organizations. And the lodging industry covered in this paper is a typical interpersonal service organization.

Aoki (2015) points out the appropriateness of considering using the extended framework of MCS as MCS in an interpersonal service organization. Specifically, "MCS as a package" by Malmi and Brown (2008) is cited. This is because the traditional MCS argument is based on Cybernetic Control (e.g., Anthony, 1965; Anthony and Govindarajan, 2007). And its main target is middle management. However, Malmi and Brown (2008) focus on "control of employee behavior" for MCS. They argue that the systems, rules, customs, values, etc., established by top management should be called MCS.

Malmi and Brown (2008) also feature cultural controls and administrative controls. Organizational culture (such as company motto and workplace design) is a control system when used to restrict behavior. In addition, administrative control functions as a system that directs employee behavior as a process that identifies the behavior itself, behavior monitoring, and whether or not to perform the behavior.

3. Data Collection: Interviews

The author has conducted several interviews with a number of companies in the lodging industries. These interviews revealed that not many companies are strongly aware of productivity in the lodging industry. These interviews conducted so far have shown that productivity is strongly recognized in a small number of lodging companies, and that these companies have their own performance indexes. Unfortunately, it is a confidential matter of this company, so its contents cannot be shown here. However, according to interviews conducted so far, only one company responded that they were strongly aware of productivity.

So what are other companies in the lodging and industry aware of? Is it unnecessary to be aware of productivity?

Speaking of the index values emphasized in the lodging industry, many respondents answered Average Daily (room) Rate (ADR), and Occupancy. In addition, there are many cases where RevPAR, Revenue per Available Room, which is the product of these and represents the profitability of the guest room department in the lodging industry, is added to this answer. Of course, values such as sales and profits are also emphasized.

For reference, if we turn our eyes to the Food and Beverage industry, there are many responses that indicate the ratio of food materials cost and FL cost ratio (the ratio of Food costs and Labor costs in sales). In some cases, index values such as the unit price of guests, the occupancy rate of seats, the turnover rate of seats, and the values of these by time zones (breakfast, lunch, dinner, night, midnight, etc.) are added.[1]

4. Discussions

In examining the impact and effectiveness of MCS on the productivity of the lodging industry, two examples will be presented. One is a Luxury hotel and the other is a Business (Budget) hotel. For any hotel, we would

---

[1] A 24-hour restaurant divides time zones into six, and calculates index values for each time zone. "Morning" means the time zone from 6am to 10am, "Lunch" from 10am to 2pm, "Idle" from 2pm to 6pm, "Dinner" from 2pm to 10pm, "Night" from 10pm to 2am, "Midnight" from 2am to 6am the next day. And from 6am to 6am next day is "One day" for this restaurant.

like to consider the knowledge gained when the author stayed or conducted an interview with the management.

4.1 *Discussion 1: Luxury hotel*

Here is an example of what happened at the Ritz-Carlton Hotel. Based on this example, we will examine how MCS can improve productivity.

According to Yoshioka (2015), Ritz-Carlton grants US$2,000 per day to all employees. If it is for the service to guests, each employee can freely make a decision up to that amount without asking others, even their boss, to make a decision.

In The Ritz-Carlton in Osaka, Japan, when a guest checked out, he forgot his lecture manuscript and glasses which he was to use in the afternoon on that day. The guest noticed what he forgot on the bullet train and immediately called the hotel. The cleaning staff who received this phone call found the manuscript and glasses in the room, said, "I will immediately follow you by the Shinkansen, the bullet train". So she left the hotel and got on the Shinkansen, met the guest at Tokyo Station, handed over the manuscript and glasses, and returned to the hotel where she worked by the Shinkansen again.

Traveling between this hotel and Tokyo Station by the Shinkansen takes about 6 hours and about 27,000 yen (about US$253) for transportation for a round trip. The cleaning staff carried out this action without anybody's approval.

This event had an advertising effect on that day and after. Because the guest talked about this event in the lecture on that day. This event is well known to those interested in the lodging industry. In fact, the author often talk about this in lectures and other situations.

This example will be examined based on the cultural and administrative controls of Malmi and Brown (2008). It can be said that the approval of US$2,000 per day for workplace design made this event possible. Moreover, it can be said that this action was performed as a service for the guests. In other words, it can be said that MCS as a package as defined by Malmi and Brown (2008) worked.

As mentioned above, there are many people who have come to know The Ritz-Carlton through this event. This can be said to have increased the number of guests.

As another example from The Ritz-Carlton, I will introduce how reservation mistakes are dealt with. This is an example of what the former Japanese branch president of this hotel told on a TV program.

One day, a patron visited the hotel to stay. But no reservation had been made at the hotel. To be precise, a reservation had been made for the same date but for a year later. In other words, some mistake had been made when making the reservation. As the patron was a regular customer who always stayed in expensive rooms, neglecting this customer would have a negative effect in the future, of course. So, the former Japanese branch president confirmed that there was an equivalent room in a nearby hotel, but in fact no room was available anywhere.

However, there was a hotel where only one room was available. But this room was under renovation, only half of it could be used. The other half was being renovated. That hotel offered to let out the room for an amount of US$ 2,000 per night. As that was the amount that could be used from The Ritz-Carlton's US$2,000 set aside to be used per day without approval from authority, the guest was told that this was the other hotel, and booked The Ritz-Carlton accommodation for the next visit.

This example can be said to prove the function of MCS as a package as described by Malmi and Brown (2008). Moreover, it can be said that the staff who acquired the repurchase and did not lose the regular customer reacted in an appropriate manner.

These two examples of The Ritz-Carlton have led to increased revenue from a long-term perspective. This is the main point in this paper. In other words, as stated in the formula for calculating labor productivity, an increase in revenue (or sales) leads to an increase in Added Value. In addition, an increase in Added Value contributes to an improvement in productivity.

In addition, in these examples, US$2,000 decision-making authority was utilized. That is, the cost has increased. However, these increased costs do not affect the Added Value. Although this increase in costs leads to a decrease in profit, the Added Value does not change.

In short, an increase in revenue due to an increase in customers (hotel guests) improves productivity.

According to interviews conducted by the author with this hotel's former Japan branch president, the US$2,000 decision-making authority plays a role that does not limit the services that the staff can provide to customers. In general, to perform any additional services, there is a corresponding cost. Even if it is one dollar, it is a cost. This decision-making authority provides staff with the possibility of providing additional services to customers, albeit at a limit of US$2,000. It can be said that this workplace design is working.

4.2 Discussion 2: Business (budget) hotel

Super Hotel is introduced as an example of the second study. Based on this example, we will examine how MCS can improve productivity.

According to Yoshioka (2015), there are many things that can be found "at a general hotel but not at Super Hotel." For example, rooms do not have telephones. There is nothing in the refrigerator in the room. There is no key to the room. The bed in the room has no legs.

The telephone in the guest room is not necessary because most guests use mobile phones. Guests also use mobile phones to contact the hotel front desk. Even if the refrigerator is empty, drinks can be purchased from vending machines in the neighborhood or the hotel. The lack of a key to a guest room means that there is no key like a metal or plastic card. There is a numeric keypad on the doorknob. In addition, the personal identification number is written on the receipt received at check-in. Guests can enter the room with this PIN code. Furthermore, when the guest returns from their visits even at midnight, they can use this PIN code for entering the hotel.

These eliminate the need for a checkout process. There is no need to pay for telephone charges because there is no need to call outside from the telephone in the guest room. Since the refrigerator is empty, there is no need to clear the drink. There is no key so there is no need to return it. As a general rule, guests should leave by 10:00 in the morning because housekeeping starts at that time every day.

In addition, this service design eliminates the need for checkout personnel during the morning hours. In fact, there is no staff at the front desk usually in the morning, even though there might be queues waiting for checkout procedure in many hotels. Labor productivity is improved because workers and working hours are no longer needed.

We can see from this example of Super Hotel that the cultural control of Malmi and Brown (2008) is working. This is because labor saving by organizational culture (workplace design) reduces the denominator in the labor productivity calculation formula, that is, the number of workers and working hours.

According to an interview with the hotel by the author and a TV program introducing this hotel, Super Hotel does not save everything. The rooms are designed to "sleep well" with a focus on guest sleep. As an example of soundproofing, the sound generated by opening and closing doors is minimized. At this hotel, which is often used for business, guests say they sleep better than when staying at other hotels. It is a measure for that.

5. Conclusion and Further Researches

This paper focuses on the lodging industry and examines the impact and effect of MCS on its productivity. In addition, the following points have been studied as research questions for that purpose.

- Will MCS in the industry play a role in building a productive system for these companies in these industries?
- How effectively and in what ways does MCS affect the industry's productivity?

This paper was examined based on MCS as a package by Aoki (2015) and Malmi and Brown (2008). As a result, it became clear that the cultural and administrative controls by Malmi and Brown (2008) played a role. This can be confirmed from the examination of the two hotels taken as examples.

On the other hand, there are many issues that still need to be addressed in this research. This paper focuses on Malmi and Brown (2008), but there is a lot of previous research on MCS. This paper only deals with some of them. In the future, I would like to continue my research on the role of MCS in the lodging industry, especially the role related to productivity improvement.

References

Anthony, R.N. (1965). *Planning and Control Systems: A Framework for Analysis*, Boston: Harvard University.

Anthony, R.N. and Govindarajan, V. (2007) *Management Control System*, New York: Irwin McGraw-Hill.

Aoki, A. (2015). Management control systems in high customer contact service organization, *Kaikei (Accounting)*, Vol. 186, No. 6, Moriyama Shoten. (In Japanese).

Japan Productivity Center (2018). *International Comparison of Labor Productivity 2018*, https://www.jpc-net.jp/intl_comparison/intl_comparison_2018.pdf (accessed 15 May 2019). (In Japanese).

Kajiura, A. (2016). Productivity components and the reality of Added Value Distribution, *Productivity Improvement Theory and Practice*, Chuo Keizai-sha. (In Japanese).

Malmi, T. and D.A. Brown (2008). Management control systems as a package — Opportunities, challenges and research directions, *Management Accounting Research*, Vol. 19, No. 4, pp. 287–300.

Mizuno, I. (2019). Basic philosophy and purpose of new added value analysis, in The Center of Productivity Comprehensive Research (ed.), *Added Value Concept Today for High Added Value Management*, Tokyo: Japan Productivity Center. (In Japanese).

Policy Research Institute, Ministry of Finance, Japan (2015). *Monthly Report of Financial Statistics* (773). (In Japanese).

Stewart, S. and Johns, N. (1996). Total quality: An approach to managing productivity in the hotel industry, in Johns, N. (ed.), *Productivity Management in Hospitality and Tourism*, New York: Cassell.

Yoshioka, T. (2015). How to provide "Good Services" — Learning from some cases of luxury hotel and budget hotel, *Communications of JIMA*, Vol. 24, No. 4, pp. 201–206, Japan Industrial Management Association. (In Japanese).

Chapter 8

Management Control System in Value Co-Creation Processes

Akimichi Aoki

Department of Business Administration, Senshu University,
Tokyo 101-8425, Japan

1. Introduction

The framework of management control has changed with the times, taking in knowledge of adjacent academic fields and newly developed management techniques. Also, the object of management control expands from the middle manager to include frontline employees, and further, it expands to the outside of the company. An example of extending the scope of application outside the company is inter-organization management control between buyers and suppliers. Though such changes and expansions will continue, it is not always excellent to change to include a wide range of contents. It is necessary to examine whether problems in the management process can be more appropriately understood by the change of the concept of management control and the extension of the application object for each topic.

As an example of the expansion of management control, this chapter focuses on the value co-creation process between a company and customers. Unlike one-way value delivery from a company to customers, interaction and communication between a company and customers would occur in value co-creation process, and context value would be generated in the

115

customer. This enhancement of the context value contributes to the value of the company. Thus, if there is a difference in the process by which corporate value is generated, the object of management control and the way it affects should be different. What are the similarities and differences between the service delivery process and value co-creation process?

Additionally, this chapter focuses on the value co-creation delivery process. The value co-creation process assumes that there is direct contact with the customer. Also, the service delivery process focuses on the management of contact with the customer (in the field of service management, the term "service encounter" is used.) to improve the quality of the service provided. Both the improvement of quality in service delivery and value creation in the service delivery process focus on contact, but how should we understand the difference between them?

2. Definitions and Characteristics of Value Co-Creation

This section discusses value co-creation with customers in the service provision process. Gronroos and Gummerus (2014) defined that value co-creation is "the process of creating something together in the process of direct interactions between two or more actors (p. 209)". Companies and customers are assumed to be service providers. It is premised that customers always participate in value creation, and the customers themselves play an essential role in the value creation process. Companies need to manage the value co-creation process with customers through management control because the value co-creation process and the evaluation of the co-created output are likely to affect the customers' re-purchase intentions.

The difference between service delivery and value co-creation in the service industry is depicted in Fig. 1. Service delivery is based on the assumption that companies and customers play different roles. The service provider (company) is a producer of service goods. The company designs the service delivery process, and service goods are delivered to customers. Though the service provider and customers contact each other in the service delivery process, customers only play the role of receiving and consuming service goods.

An example of a value creation model through value delivery in a service delivery process is an service profit chain (S-PC). S-PC is a model

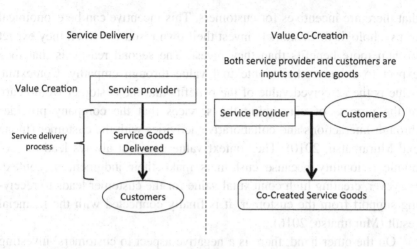

Fig. 1. The difference between value delivery and value co-creation.

developed by Heskett *et al.* (1994). They clarified the unique profit acquisition process in the service industry. According to them, the improvement
of internal service quality formed by job design, employee selection, and
compensation system enhances employee satisfaction. Finally, it leads to
the enhancement of financial performance through customer satisfaction.
Kondo (2012) characterized the model by (1) placing the starting point of
causal relationship on employee satisfaction and (2) favorable customer
responses affecting employee satisfaction. The feature of (2) is called
"satisfaction mirror." It shows the relation between customers and
employees, whereby when a customer is satisfied by an employee, the
satisfaction level of the employee who catered to the satisfied customer is
also improved. Thus, in the value delivery process, there is an interaction
between the company and the customers, and the customer's behavior has
a psychological impact on the company's employees. Although there is a
high possibility that the quality of service improves with the improvement
in employee satisfaction, S-PC is different from the value co-creation
because the customers do not put their resources into the service delivery
process.

Earlier in this chapter, it was stated that an important feature of the
value co-creation process is that the customers also put their resources into
it. So, why do customers cooperate in creating value? The first reason is

that there are incentives for customers. This incentive can be economical or psychological. Customers invest their own resources when they expect to gain more benefits than they invest. The second reason is that they expect to enhance their contextual value through empathy. Contextual value is the perceived value of the benefits that the customer would earn in the process of consuming the services that the company provides through interactions and collaborative activities with the customer (Inoue and Muramatsu, 2010). The context value does not always lead to economic rationality because customers make their judgment in context. However, creating high contextual value for the customer leads to receiving support from the customer. It is finally connected with the financial result (Muramatsu, 2016).

On the other hand, there is a negative aspect to customers' investing their resources. A problem arises when a customer who is responsible for value co-creation recognizes that the quality of the co-created output is low, despite the considerable time and effort invested in value co-creation. The expectation gap occurs, and customer dissatisfaction increases. The expectation for the quality of the output rises in the situation in which the degree of the co-creation is high. Therefore, a lack of perceived performance results in more significant disappointment with co-created services (Heidenreich *et al.*, 2015). According to Parasuraman (2006), the higher the involvement of customers in service delivery, the higher the number of contact points between customers and service providers. Increasing the number of contact points make the service delivery process more complicated and increases the likelihood of service failure.

3. Management Control System for Value Co-Creation Processes

This section compares the traditional concept with new and extended concept of management control and discusses which concept is more applicable to the process of value co-creation with customers. Although there are various definitions of management control and its scope, the most widely known definition is "the process by which managers influence other members of the organization to implement the organization's strategies" (Anthony and Govindarajan, 2007, p. 6) (hereinafter, this definition is referred to as "Anthony's framework"). In this framework, management control is based on cybernetic and formal control. The object of the control is middle management. It is clearly stated that the target of management's control is limited to the company.

Also, in "Anthony's framework," task control, which aims to realize the efficient and effective performance of individual tasks, is arranged as a subordinate concept of management control. The object of task control is lower management of the company. Lower management is assumed to perform programmed and routine activities. "Anthony's framework" assumes that task control is highly suited to the business environment in which lower management performs regular and repeated tasks (Aoki, 2017).

In contrast to the above concept, the extended concept which regards various management control systems (Mcs) as a package has recently become dominant (hereinafter, this definition is referred to as "package framework"). Malmi and Brown (2008) defined Mcs as "those systems, rules, practices, values, and other activities management puts in place in order to direct employee behavior (p. 290)." Also, they argued that there are a number of reasons why studying the Mcs package phenomenon is important (p. 287). "The concept of a package points to the fact that different systems are often introduced by different interest groups at different times, so the idea of the controls entirety should not be defined holistically as a single system, but instead as a package of systems (p. 291)". Even within the package framework, the object of management controls is employees working within the organization. However, management control and other control systems are classified according to the presence or absence of control of the action from managers (superior) to employees (subordinate), and the object of management control is extended to all employees. The approach to the frontline employee by the lower management is also included in the management control. They also stated that management controls "include all the devices and systems managers use to ensure that the behaviors and decisions of their employees are consistent with organization's objectives and strategies, but exclude pure decision support systems (pp. 290–291)." The components of management control of "package framework" are widely extended compared to "Anthony's framework."

Also, Merchant and Van der Stede (2017) defined management control to "include everything managers do to help ensure that their organization's strategies and plans are carried out or, if conditions warrant, that they are modified (p. xii)." They also showed four control systems: (1) control by results (results controls), (2) control by behavior (action controls), (3) personnel controls, and (4) control by culture (cultural controls). They assume that the target is also employees, but the expansion of the object and components of management accounting are applicable to research on management control in value co-creation with customers. With these conceptual changes and expansion, lower management approaches to frontline employees and customers for value co-creation can also be included in management control concepts.

A significant challenge in interpersonal service and value co-creation is to guide the behavior of frontline employees, who need to confront customers directly and act flexibly, in the desired direction for the organization. These actions by superiors are diverse and should be understood in the context of management control, not task control.

Whether it is a one-way service delivery or a value co-creation process, managers can not intervene in the actions of subordinates involved in the service encounter. Thus, in addition to cybernetic control, such as budgetary control, managers indirectly control employee behavior through corporate philosophy, organizational culture, or principles of practices. In service organizations, they attempt to permeate the sense of values by their credo, and the introduction of the principles for action is carried out. These function as Mcs. In the service delivery process, the control by policy and procedure works effectively for the routine works, and the control by culture works effectively for the deviation from the predetermined procedure. Such cultural or administrative controls are essential in the Mcs of interpersonal organizations.

Since value co-creation is implemented through contact with customers, management of service encounter is important in human service organizations. According to Muramatsu (2016), there are three ways to influence the context value of customers through the service encounter: (1) the improvement of the quality of the service encounter directly affects the customer's consumption process, (2) the quality of the service encounter indirectly affects the customer's consumption process after the service is delivered, and (3) customers are affected by the information transmission and the joint involvement of service goods based on the service encounter. To enhance the context value, the quality of service encounter should be improved. These requirements have much in common with those for delivering high-quality services.

As we can see from the examples mentioned above, not all customers want to create value together. In addition to collecting information in advance, it is essential for frontline employees in charge of service encounter to search for customer preferences. In practice, there will not be two different types of customers, but customer behavior will vary depending on the situation. For example, even during a stay at a hotel, it is conceivable to act in a manner that promotes value co-creation for one event and to act in a value co-creation manner only by receiving service for another event.

Will the components and objects of Mcs change in the environment of value co-creation? As the importance of service encounters increases, more attention will be paid to Mcs to guide frontline employees directly or indirectly in the desired direction. Also, focusing on the improvement of context value, the importance of cultural control for frontline employees will increase. This is because customers improve their context value through long-term contact with the employees by understanding the value and organizational culture of the company more deeply. On the other hand, for the employees in charge of service encounter, results controls are also necessary because the enhancement of the context value of the customer often does not have economic rationality.

The context value of the customer is enhanced by controlling the behavior of the customer. The approach to the action of the customer is limited in the means, and the coercive force is also weak. Cybernetic control cannot be applied to customers. Therefore, the means would be limited to cultural control. To enhance the context value recognized by the customer, it is crucial that the customer knows the service of the company well and that the company controls the expected value of the customer accurately. Failure in managing this expectation can lead to failure in value co-creation.

In Fig. 2, there are two types of control systems: management control and encouragement of external customers. Companies need to design

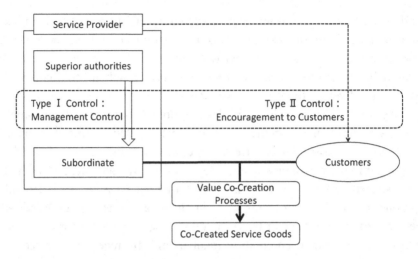

Fig. 2.   Mcs in the value co-creation environment.

Mcs with two points in mind: (1) consistency of Mcs from superior to subordinate and (2) consistency of control both internally (employees) and externally (customer). Control of customer behavior is an attempt to enhance context value.

4. Case: XYZ Company

4.1 *Overview of XYZ company*

This section discusses value co-creation with customers and Mcs in the Business Partner Department of XYZ company. XYZ company was founded in 2012 in Japan, with about 500 employees (as of the end of June 2019). The company sells cloud-based accounting software. Due to the nature of the business model of Software as a Service (SaaS), XYZ company delivers service continuously to existing customers even after the contract to purchase the service. The quality of the interaction between the company and customers affects the customer lifetime value of the service. The Business Partner Department is a department that provides the product (software) to the offices of accounting professionals such as Certified Public Accountants (CPAs) and Tax Accountants (TAs). The department consists of Sales Team, Customer Success Team, and Marketing Team. Community Team, which is a part of Marketing Team, creates value with customers through interaction and engagement with existing customers.

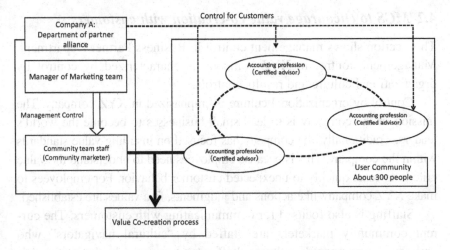

Fig. 3.   Value co-creation by Business Partner Department.

Figure 3 shows how Business Partnership Department co-creates value with customers. The main customers of the department are professional accounting firms. XYZ company builds the user community to use its services. The user community has about 300 members of the accounting profession in five areas of the country. The company's marketing team is staffed by "community marketers" who work with customers (members of the community) online and offline daily.

The role of community marketers is as follows. The first role is to increase the customers' calorific value through dialogue with the customer (online and offline) and regular off-line events and to contribute to the value enhancement of the company's products and services. As a result, customers are expected to propagate the company's products to potential customers. The second role is to collect requests of customers (Certified Advisors) and reflect them in the improvement of existing products and the development of new products.

The expected role for customers is to act in the community to improve XYZ company's services. A high-quality community is an essential component of product value from the customers' point of view. As community marketers interact with their customers to improve the quality of their communities, the quality of the services they provide will also develop. Therefore, management control in the company and approach to the customer outside the company are carried out to enhance the quality of value co-creation.

4.2 *MCS to encourage value co-creation with customers*

This section shows management control in Business Partner Department. Management control in XYZ company is characterized by control by organizational culture and results controls.

Control by organizational culture is emphasized in XYZ company. The mission of the company is to lead small businesses to become the world's leaders. Traditionally, the company has focused on instilling value standards within the company. This is because employees need to understand the value criteria to react quickly to unexpected customer behavior. For employees to make XYZ company-like actions and judgments, five values are established.

Staffing is also focused for communicating with customers. The current community marketers are staffed by "cultural navigators" who embody the company's culture. Staff who can embody the company's values will be responsible for interacting with customers, increasing the likelihood of value co-creation along the organizational culture. A certain percentage of the budget (discretionary costs) is allocated to marketing over the medium to long term.

4.3 *Results Controls*

As measures for implementing management control for the value co-creation process, XYZ company sets several key performance indicators (KPIs) every quarter. KPIs are (1) the number of participants for each event, (2) the ratio of new customers to the total number of participants for each event, and (3) the return on investments (ROI). Community team staff frequently share these numbers with their bosses. The result of KPIs is not only used for reporting, but also as a communication tool for future predictions such as why the results were obtained and how the next numerical figures are likely to change. These figures are not linked to individual evaluations and compensation.

4.4 *Approaches to external customers*

The Business Partner Department manages the user community jointly with customers. Therefore, it is crucial to approach customers. The approach to customers is not based on financial incentives. XYZ company expects customers to empathize and act with the company's values and organizational culture. Many customers are sympathetic not only to the company's products but also to its mission and values. Customers receive psychological rewards such as opportunities to express themselves through community management.

Since XYZ company does not reward its customers (Certified Advisors) based on external incentives, it does not pay customers for community operations. As an incentive for customers, there is a monitoring system for new products and new functions. They can review new functions in cooperation with engineers and can know in advance new functions which will be installed shortly. This monitoring system has an advantage that customers also have the consciousness of being a "buddy" sharing the mission.

The approach to the customer emphasizes the encouragement of voluntary action. XYZ company believes that urging voluntary action by customers is more important than forcing the action from the customers. If employees get too involved with the user community, customers will lose their sense of ownership. When community marketers want to give advice, they have to endure a lot.

5. Conclusion

This chapter examined the design and operation of Mcs for value co-creation with customers implemented in the service delivery process. Though the value co-creation with the customer can be implemented in the service organization, this chapter identified that it was essential to carry out the design, including human resource development and organization design. Notably, it is important to prepare the conditions for enhancing the context value of customers.

As to Mcs in the value co-creation process, it is desirable to recognize management control in a more extended approach. Because the object of management control in the value co-creation is employees who directly contact the customer, not the middle management. Also, since control by culture is considered to be effective in co-creation with customers, it seems to be useful to grasp the means of management control widely.

This chapter also examined the what points were emphasized in the execution of the value co-creation. The result measures were not used for diagnostic control but were mainly used for grasping the present state and searching for the problem. This does not mean that performance measurement is not essential. Another department of the company strictly uses financial control, such as budgetary control for management control. Result measures were used exploratively to implement the value co-creation effectively.

On the other hand, cultural control was critical in the value co-creation of the company. And, it was clarified that the organization structure and personnel allocation were also carried out so that the control by the culture may function adequately.

The culture mainly controlled the approach to customers. The consistency of management control for employees as well as customers was recognized. We can see the possibility for new extensions of management control in terms of (1) consistency of Mcs from superior to subordinate and (2) consistency of control both internally (employees) and externally (customer).

References

Anthony, R.N. and Govindarajan, V. (2007). *Management Control Systems*, (12th edition), Boston: McGraw-Hill.

Aoki, A. (2017). The new direction of management control theory in service organizations, *The Journal of Management Accounting,* Vol. 25, No. 2, pp. 19–33. (in Japanese.)

Gronroos, C. and Gummerus, J. (2014). The service revolution and its marketing implications: Service logic vs service dominant logic, *Marketing Service Quality,* Vol. 24, No. 3, pp. 206–229.

Heidenreich, S.K. Wittkowski, M. *et al.* (2015). The dark side of customer co-creation: Exploring the consequences of failed co-created services, *Journal of the Academy of Marketing Science,* Vol. 43, pp. 279–296.

Heskett, J.L., Jones, T.O. *et al.* (1994). Putting the service-profit chain to work, *Harvard Business Review,* Vol. 72, No. 2, pp. 164–174.

Inoue, T. and Muramatsu, J. (2010). *Service Dominant Logic,* Tokyo: Dobunkan Publishing (Japanese).

Kondo, T. (2012). *The Theory and Method of Service Innovation,* Tokyo: Productivity Publishing (Japanese).

Malmi, T. and Brown, D.A. (2008). Management control systems as a package — opportunities, challenges and research directions, *Management Accounting Research*, Vol. 19, No. 4, pp. 287–300.

Merchant, K.A. and *Van der Stade, W.A.* (2012). *Management Control Systems: Performance Measurement, Evaluation and Incentives*, 4th edition. Harlow: FT Prentice Hall.

Muramatsu, J. (2016). *Casebook: Vale Co-Creation and Marketing*, Tokyo: Dobunkan Publishing (Japanese).

Parasuraman, A. (2006). Modeling opportunities in service recovery and customer-managed interactions, *Marketing Science*, Vol. 25, No. 6, pp. 590–593.

Part 3

Other Topics

Chapter 9

Excessive Quality in the Japanese Laundry Industry

Zhi Wang

Faculty of Economics, Sophia University,
Tokyo 102-8554, Japan

1. Introduction

Quality control is one of the methods of cost management (Wang, 2009). Previous literature in management accounting and production control focused on quality defects that occur when the quality is lower than customer requirements and the costs or losses related to the quality defects (Ito, 2005; Kajiwara, 2008; Horngren *et al.*, 2008; Juran, 1951; Feigenbaum, 1961; Crosby, 1979). However, as described later in this chapter, the quality provided by an organization may be below or above customer requirements. It is not sufficient to examine quality only from the aspect of quality defects.

This chapter defines excessive quality as that which exceeds customer requirements. In other words, the quality provided by an organization and the quality requested by the customer are compared, and if the former exceeds the latter, the gap is regarded as excessive quality. There are studies on excessive quality (Albright and Roth, 1992; Ito, 2005), but it has not been fully explained, specifically, as the cause of excessive quality and its effects on cost. Excessive quality is now a significant problem in business practice. For instance, in the service industry, which accounts for

131

approximately 70% of Japan's GDP, quality tends to be excessive and expensive in many fields according to the 2009 and 2017 survey conducted by the Japan Productivity Center.

The purpose of this chapter is to clarify the causes of excessive quality and its effects on cost. In the following sections, a literature review is first presented, and the research question is established. Based on the study of Kikuya Co., Ltd, a company that operates a laundry business, this chapter analyzes the company-provided quality and customer-requested quality. That is, some customers need laundry services promptly, and some do not, and this chapter discusses the causes of excessive quality and its pertinence.

2. Research Review and Research Questions

2.1 Management accounting research

In management accounting and production control, a number of studies have been performed on quality, and commonly, quality is classified into the quality of conformance and quality of design. Examples of such studies in management accounting include Ito (2005), Kajiwara (2008) and Horngren *et al.* (2008), and those in production control include Juran (1951), Feigenbaum (1961), and Crosby (1979).

Quality of conformance is defined as a fit between the attributes of an actual product and its specifications. In the production process, the equipment and materials for ensuring the quality of design are determined, and it is unlikely that the quality of conformance exceeds the quality of design. On the other hand, due to the influence of process conditions, quality of conformance may deviate from the quality of design, resulting in quality defects. Quality defects are attracting attention as though they were gold in the mines (Juran, 1951), and if eliminated, directly lead to an increase in corporate profits. Also, management accounting helps resolve quality defects that occur during the production process since it specializes in cost and efficiency of production. That is the reason why there are many studies on quality defects in management accounting.

Quality of design is defined as a fit between customer requirements and product specifications. There may be a gap between the two due to an inaccurate grasp of customer requirements. Excessive quality occurs when the specifications exceed customer requirements (Albright and Roth,

1992; Ito, 2005). Excessive quality of design can be grasped by target costing, although it is difficult with conventional management accounting methods. In target costing, a functional cost analysis of components is performed based on customer requirements obtained from market research, and target costs (allowable cost) of the component or function are set and compared to the attainable costs (Ansari *et al.*, 1997). The quality of a component or function is excessive when the attainable cost exceeds the target cost.

Quality of conformance and quality of design are the physical aspects of the quality set by the engineer based on customer requirements. The previous literature focused on the physical aspects of quality. In recent years, research on the application of target costing in the service industry (Okada, 2007; Tanimori and Tasaka, 2013; Kondo, 2017) has been increasing. For example, Tanimori and Tasaka (2013) examined the applicability of target costing for ATM functions in banks, and Kondo (2017) examined restaurant menu development, such as purchasing ingredients. However, these studies still focused on the physical aspects of quality.

Quality is considered to be a customer requirement. Quality should not be limited only to the physical nature of the product or service, but the delivery process may also be considered a component. An example of this is responsiveness. Responsiveness defines rapidity as the response time that service providers take to provide service to customers (Parasuraman *et al.*, 1988). SERVQUAL and SERVPERF measure service quality in service marketing and responsiveness is one of the components of quality. Therefore, quality in this study includes the process of providing the products and services.

2.2 *Service marketing research*

In service marketing, there are many research results on service quality (Fisk *et al.*, 1993). In the 1980s, based on the expectation-disconfirmation theory (Oliver, 1980), the research defined service quality by the gap between customer expectations and perceptions (Grönroos, 2007), and SERVQUAL was proposed (Parasuraman *et al.*, 1988). In the 1990s, problems such as ambiguity of expectations in SERVQUAL were identified (Cronin and Taylor, 1992), and SERVPERF, consisting only of perceived quality, was created. SERVQUAL and SERVPERF use the same five dimensions (tangibles, reliability, responsiveness, assurance and empathy) and 22 items to measure service quality.

It is said that more or higher quality should be provided (Cronin and Taylor, 1992; Estelami and Maeyer, 2002), and services that exceed customer expectations have a positive impact on customer satisfaction and delight (Estelami and Maeyer, 2002; Oliver *et al.*, 1997). Excessiveness often leads to an adverse consumer reaction caused by providing more service than necessary (Estelami and Maeyer, 2002; Ku *et al.*, 2013). In other words, even if the service exceeds customer requirements, it is only regarded as excessive quality if there is an adverse reaction.

2.3 *Research questions*

Management accounting research can supplement the efficiency of service provision, which is lacking in marketing research. For instance, in target costing, comparing the allowable cost with the target cost may reveal that the allowable cost is too high and leads to a cost reduction.

In target costing, cost reduction is achieved through quality control. The excessive quality of design causes costs to be higher than necessary. It is possible to capture excessive quality by examining the differences in quality. That is, it is possible to compare the importance of the customer-requested component with the importance of the company-provided component (Ansari *et al.*, 1997, pp. 140–158; Okamoto, 2000, pp. 857–874).

Based on the knowledge of discovering excessive quality of design in target costing, this study compares the customer-requested quality with company-provided quality to detect excessive quality and then confirms its effects on cost. The following research questions are established:

1. Has excessive quality occurred in the process of service provision?
2. What causes excessive quality in the process of service provision?
3. What are the effects of excessive quality on cost?

3. Research Design

3.1 *Methodology*

This study uses the laundry industry as a research subject. Due to the impact of the evolution of household washing machines and detergents,

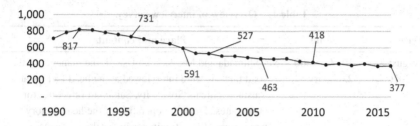

Fig. 1. Market size of general consumer laundry by year (unit: billion yen).

and the trend toward casual fashion, the general consumer laundry market in Japan has been declining. The market reached a peak of 817.0 billion yen in 1992 and decreased to less than half of the peak in 2016 to 376.7 billion yen (Fig. 1, http://www.nicli.co.jp, *Japan Cleaning Journal*). It faces a very harsh management environment, and eliminating waste and efficient management are essential issues for survival. Nevertheless, there is excessive quality in the industry, which is described later. Therefore, the laundry industry is a good example when considering excessive quality that is often overlooked.

The purpose of this study is to understand better what factors cause excessive quality and its effect on costs in a circumstance where there is little research. Therefore, this study uses a field study rather than questionnaires targeting large numbers of samples. While investigating excessive quality in the laundry industry, the situation in Kikuya was selected as it most closely related to the problem at hand.

3.2 Data collection

The data used in this study includes the articles written by Yoshiaki Shimada (Shimada, 2010, 2015), vice president of Kikuya, and Shinichi Nakahata (Nakahata, 2013, 2016), the representative director, and a field study. After understanding the company's situation to some extent through the literature, this study conducted three rounds of semi-structured interviews (Table 1). For accuracy, the interview contents were recorded and documented with the consent of interviewees. Moreover, before the contents of the interview were published, the manuscript was sent to the interviewees in advance and was confirmed by them.

Mr. Shimada, who changed roles from a production control position in manufacturing to a position at Kikuya in February 2001, was selected as the

Table 1.   Overview of interview survey.

Date	Time	Place and contents
August 2, 2016	10:00–12:00 2.0 hours	Mr. Shimada and Ms. Kiyoko Usami, the manager of the head factory, were interviewed at the head factory at Yatsukagamicho, Soka City, Saitama Prefecture, for 90 minutes. Then, the operation of the head factory was observed for 30 minutes under the guidance of Mr. Shimada.
September 22, 2017	13:30–15:00 1.5 hours	Mr. Shimada was interviewed at the head factory for 90 minutes.
April 9, 2018	13:30–16:30 3.0 hours	After interviewing Mr. Shimada for 80 minutes at the head factory, the Matsufushi factory and clothing storage warehouse at Matsufushi-cho, Kitakatsushika-gun, Saitama Prefecture were visited for 70 minutes. * Travel time between the factories was 30 minutes.

interviewee. The reason for this is that based on his experience, he was aware of the excess in the process of service provision. Additionally, he was a vice president and participated in the decision-making of business execution and was familiar with the overall view of the company. Mr. Shimada indicated the excess equipment and increased labor costs (Shimada, 2010) but did not use the term excessive quality. Therefore, in the interview survey, to avoid projecting the interviewer's way of thinking on the interviewee, the term excess was used rather than excessive quality.

4. Case Study

4.1 *Case introduction*

Established in 1956, Kikuya has used the chain method to increase the number of stores since 1965. As of September 2017, the headquarters is located in Adachi City, a ward of Tokyo. There are two factories[1] in Saitama Prefecture and over 90 stores in the Tokyo metropolitan area with

---

[1] As of September 2017, Kikuya had two factories. The change from three factories held in 2010 to two factories is the effect of the shrinking laundry cleaning market (interview on September 22, 2017).

approximately 175 employees. Kikuya also established a subsidiary in Bangkok, Thailand, in 2013, and had 22 stores in Thailand as of September 2017. Domestic sales in 2016 were around 1,130 million yen, and sales in Thailand were over 100 million yen. The company launched its home delivery laundry service (www.reaqua.jp) in 2015 and won the Excellence Award at the Japan Service Awards in 2016 hosted by the institution of Japan Service Productivity & Innovation for Growth.

4.2 Case result

4.2.1 Quality provided by the company

In order to enhance customer satisfaction, Kikuya sent the clothes received from the customers to the factory immediately, regardless of the season, or whether it was a weekend or weekday, and returned them to the stores as soon as they were finished at the factory. In the second half of the 1990s, Kikuya built a system that allowed items received by 12:00 noon to be delivered the next day (Shimada, 2010).

Next day delivery is not straightforward because the clothes must be tagged and washed promptly on the same day and shipped back by the next day (Shimada, 2015). Laundry work is mostly seasonal and customer demand peaks in spring and autumn, which are seasonal changes of clothing, and decreases in summer and winter (Shimada, 2010). Moreover, Nakahata (2016) illustrated in more detail that the peak is from around April to early May, the off-season is around late February, and the former is about 14 times busier than the latter. There are more clothes received for laundering on weekends than on weekdays (Shimada, 2010).

Kikuya has been working to achieve next day delivery. If an inventory could be utilized to fulfill customer demand, next day delivery would not be difficult. However, since the recipients of the laundry service are customers' possessions, that is not possible. As Shimada (2015) explained, laundry is an equipment industry, and in order to finish the received clothes at one time, Kikuya has developed large-capacity machines according to the peak of the number of clothes received.[2]

---

[2]Kikuya attempted to return the clothes the next day, but it was difficult during peak seasons. In the case that the store could not return the clothes the next day, the store informed

4.2.2 *Quality requested by the customer*

Does Kikuya need to finish all the clothes by the next day? According to a customer survey conducted by Kikuya in 2001, the next day's pick-up rate was only about 20% (Shimada, 2010). Nakahata (2016) spoke in more detail about the content of the survey and stated, "as a result of the survey regarding the customer-requested delivery date, the options for delivery next day, two days later, three days later and one week later were each chosen by approximately 20% of the customers, and the remaining 20% chose anytime delivery. So not every customer requests a prompt delivery" (p. 20).

4.2.3 *Occurrence of excessive quality of service*

The fact that the next day's pick-up rate is only about 20% means that the customer will not come to pick up 80% of the finished clothes the next day. That is, 80% of the finished clothes were not needed by the next day, and the prompt laundry service provided to this 80% of the clothing exceeds customer requirements. Therefore, excessive quality of service occurred.

There are five dimensions of service quality: tangibles, reliability, responsiveness, assurance, and empathy (Parasuraman *et al.*, 1988). As mentioned earlier, responsiveness defines rapidity as the response time that service providers take to provide service to customers. Excessive quality of service occurred at Kikuya related to the responsiveness.

4.3 *Case discussion*

4.3.1 *The causes of excessive quality*

There was a gap between the quality provided by Kikuya and customer requirements. Since Kikuya made efforts to close the gap later, it could be

---

the customer of the earliest delivery date. The store always tried to return the clothes as quickly as possible. Mr. Shimada stated the following:

> The unwashed clothes would accumulate at the factory during the busy periods and be washed according to the tag on which the received date is written. That is, the staff went to the place where the unwashed clothes are stored, took the earliest out, and washed them. The factory informed the stores of how many days it would take (interview on September 22, 2017).

deduced that the gap was not intentionally created. If the customer's request for the delivery date is confirmed at the store upon the reception of the clothing, such a gap would not exist. It is assumed that Kikuya has not confirmed the customer's request. Mr. Shimada stated the following:

> I am from the manufacturing industry, and it was natural for me to ask customers their desired delivery date. But I think it was a little difficult for Kikuya's employees to accept it. Anyway, they never discussed the delivery date (interview on September 22, 2017).

Even if the requested pick-up date of the customer is not identified, excessive quality may be noticed through the abundant amount of washed clothes remaining at the store. As described in what follows, Kikuya did not overlook these remaining clothes. In order to solve this problem, Kikuya introduced a discount fee to customers who picked up their laundry the next day. The discount service attracted customers who were initially not thinking about picking up their laundry the next day, so it could be useful in reducing remaining clothes. However, customers who are not thinking of coming to pick up their laundry the next day are, in other words, customers who do not need the clothes the next day. Therefore, the discount service arbitrarily raised the quality level required by the customer while maintaining the company-provided quality level and tended to encourage, rather than eliminate, excessive quality of service.

> The washed clothes remaining at the store occupied store space, and delivery became complicated. To address these issues, Kikuya gave a discount to customers who picked up their laundry the next day. (Shimada, 2010, 13).

Kikuya washed all the received clothes without identifying the customer's request. Kikuya decided the delivery date and created the illusion that the customer wanted their clothes back promptly (Shimada, 2010). Mr. Shimada stated the following:

> In the manufacturing industry, the designated delivery date is identified first. The information regarding when and how many units to produce came from the headquarters, and then the shop floor started to make material plans and process plans accordingly. However, in the laundry industry, the

customer's request for a delivery date was not identified. The fact that the delivery date was set by the company was not well understood. At the time I came to Kikuya, there was a tag on the returned bag from the stores, and the only thing written on the tag was when it was received. There was no information about when to return the clothes (interview on September 22, 2017).

Why did this illusion occur? Mr. Shimada stated the following:

Production and consumption are basically simultaneous, as laundry is a service industry. All the received clothes have customers. The work is like that of a barber, who has to cut the hair of all people in the order in which they came [into the store]. Barbers do not bother to order their customers and do not do the laundry (interview on September 22, 2017).

In other words, because it is a service industry, the inseparability of production and consumption (Zeithaml *et al.*, 1985) is considered.

Another possible cause of excessive quality is the ambiguity in inventory control. Although the clothes were not owned by the company, they were handled as inventory. The fact that such a contradiction has not surfaced indicates the ambiguity in inventory control. Furthermore, the idea that inventory is bad is activated. To reduce the amount of inventory, Kikuya tried to return the clothes promptly.

In the laundry industry, inventory is ambiguous. Of course, hangers, vinyl covers, detergents, and various tags are recognized as material inventory. However, are the clothes received from the customers inventory? For sure, they are not included in the factory income statement. The fact that the contradiction of handling clothes as inventory had not surfaced earlier shows that production control is not sufficient. When the clothes are handled as inventory, the idea that inventory is bad is activated. In order to reduce inventory, the clothes are returned to the stores by the next day (Shimada, 2010, pp. 11–12).

As described above, there are two main reasons for excessive quality of service at Kikuya. The first is that Kikuya has an illusion that the customer wants the clothes back immediately, so the delivery date is not identified. The second is the ambiguity in inventory control.

4.3.2 *Detecting excessive quality of service*

Kikuya noticed the consequences of providing excessive quality, that is, a large amount of washed clothes remaining, but did not recognize the real cause of excessive quality as it was not easily perceived.

The findings of this study suggest two ways to find excessive quality of service. The first is to check the company-provided and customer-requested quality levels and compare the two. The second is to check the volume of washed clothes remaining at the store.

4.3.3 *Effects of cost reduction*

Management resources, such as large-capacity machines and a labor force, have been constructed according to the peak of the number of clothes received. However, if only the necessary clothes are cleaned immediately, the burden on various management resources will be eased. Machine capacity may be calculated as (number of machines) × (number of shifts) × (utilization) × (efficiency). If providing appropriate service, the number of machines could be reduced. Mr. Shimada stated, "this method results in a huge machine and excessive equipment." (Shimada, 2010, p. 12). The provision of excessive quality of service caused the waste of capital investment, running costs (maintenance costs, power charges, etc.), and labor costs due to overtime work in the busy periods.

In order to eliminate excessive quality, Kikuya identified a customer-requested pick-up date at the end of 2001. Also, in 2002, it introduced the storage service whereby it received clothes in the spring and stored them until the seasons changed in the fall and washed them when having surplus capacity. As a result, the amount of processing is leveled not only weekly but also annually, the operation is stabilized, and the burden on various management resources is reduced.

During the period from 2001 to 2010, the market for general consumer laundry decreased by about 21%, but Kikuya's sales only decreased by 14% (Fig. 2). It can be assumed that the methods introduced to

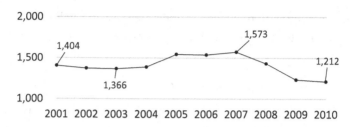

Fig. 2. Kikuya's sales trend by year (unit: million yen).

eliminate excessive quality did not impair customer satisfaction and sales. During the same period, Kikuya achieved a significant reduction in production capacity. Of the five factories that Kikuya held in 2000, two were shut down as of 2010: one was small, and the other was reasonably large. Further, the labor cost was reduced by about 30% by reducing overtime (interview on August 2, 2016).

5. Applications

5.1 *Application to the practice*

The essential characteristics of services are categorized as intangibility, inseparability, heterogeneity, and perishability. However, the laundry service is performed at the factory, and production and consumption are separated. The laundry industry tends to be an operational business model, so it may be difficult to generalize the results of this study to the entire service industry.

When considering whether or not to provide prompt service, the customer's demand is an essential factor, but at the same time, the attributes of the recipient of the service must also be considered. The recipient of the service at the store is a person, and at the factory, the recipients are the clothes. There is a time lag between receiving the clothes and delivering them, but the recipients of the laundry service are the clothes, not people, so there is no problem in extending that lag time.

It is helpful to note that Lovelock (1983) and Kotler and Armstrong (1989) classified services according to whether customers need to be present or not (Table 2). Under this framework, the results of this study are

Table 2. The nature of service act.

Who or What is the direct recipient of the service?		
	People	**Things**
Tangible actions	Services directed at people's bodies: • health care • passenger transportation • beauty salons • exercise clinics • restaurants • haircutting	Services directed at goods and other physical possessions[3]: • freight transportation • industrial equipment repair and maintenance • janitorial services • laundry and dry cleaning • landscaping/lawn care
Intangible actions	Services directed at people's minds: • education • broadcasting • information services • theaters • museums	Services directed at intangible assets: • banking • legal services • accounting • securities • insurance

particularly applicable when providing services directed to goods and other physical possessions.

5.2 *Application to the research*

In management accounting and production control, many studies on quality have focused on the aspect of insufficient quality (quality defects) and the costs or losses related to the quality defects. This study paid attention to the aspect of excessive quality and found what caused it. It showed that it was possible to reduce the costs by eliminating excessive quality, and this could be regarded as a new method of cost management. That is, increasing service productivity by reducing investment of management

---

[3]In the framework presented by Loverock (1983), the section of services directed at goods and other physical possessions includes veterinary care. Pets and livestock are living creatures that may cause problems if kept waiting. Veterinary care was excluded because the results of this study might not be applicable.

resources. As mentioned in the introduction to this chapter, the service is excessive and expensive in many fields in the Japanese service industry, so the findings from this study are expected to contribute to future research.

There may be a question of whether the findings from this study are really novel. The just-in-time (JIT) production system is well known for processing what is needed, when it is needed, and in the amount needed. JIT can be useful in eliminating excessive quality. However, the previous literature has focused on JIT's effects of reducing defective products, as described below. In that sense, this study implies new academic significance of JIT.

> Manufacturing costs are reduced due to the reduction of wasteful costs that become obvious through inventory control. For example, the manufacturing cost of defective products has been eliminated. ...Cost reduction is the most important goal, but in order to achieve this goal, the other three sub-goals have to be achieved. ...The second one [sub-goals, ed.] is quality assurance, so that each process supplies only non-defective products to the subsequent processes (Monden, 1991, pp. 54–55).

6. Conclusion

By focusing on the responsiveness (rapidity) of the service provision, which was not discussed as quality in the conventional management accounting and production control literature, this study examined the reason that caused excessive quality and its effects on cost.

In the fields of management accounting and production control, most of the literature on quality focuses on quality defects and the costs or losses related to the quality defects. However, this study considered quality control from the aspect of excessive quality. Based on the study of Kikuya, this study clarified how to detect excessive quality and presented two methods. One is to compare the quality provided by the company and the quality requested by the customer, and the other is to check the amount of washed clothes remaining at the store. Also, this study argued that cost reduction could be achieved by eliminating excessive quality of service.

The application of this study is primarily for the industry that provides services directed to goods and other physical possessions. From the viewpoint of management accounting, it means performing cost reduction by directly managing the customer's request.

References

Albright, T.L. and Roth, H.P. (1992). The measurement of quality costs: An alternative paradigm, *Accounting Horizons*, Vol. 16, No. 2, pp. 15–17.

Ansari, S.L., Bell, J.E. *et al.* (1997). *Target Costing: The Next Frontier in Strategic Cost Management*, Chicago: Irwin.

Cronin, J.J. Jr. and Taylor, S.A. (1992). Measuring service quality: A reexamination and extension, *Journal of Marketing*, Vol. 56, July, pp. 55–68.

Crosby, P.B. (1979). *Quality is Free: The Art of Making Quality Certain*, New York: New American Library.

Estelami, H. and De Maeyer, P. (2002). Customer reactions to service provider overgenerosity, *Journal of Service Research*, Vol. 4, No. 3, pp. 205–216.

Feigenbaum, A.V. (1961). *Total Quality Control*. London: McGraw-Hill.

Fisk, R., Brown, W. *et al.* (1993). Tracking the evolution of the services marketing literature, *Journal of Retailing*, Vol. 69, No. 1, pp. 61–103.

Grönroos, C. (2007). *Service Management and Marketing: Customer Management in Service Competition*, 3rd edition. Chichester: Wiley.

Horngren, C.T., Datar, S.M. *et al.* (2008). *Cost Accounting: A Management Emphasis*, 13th edition. Pearson: Prentice–Hall.

Ito, Y. (2005). *Construction and Strategic Operation of Quality Cost Management System*, Tokyo: JUSE Press. (In Japanese.)

Japan Productivity Center (2009). A comparative study between Japan and the US regarding differences in quality levels in the service sectors, in Hiromatsu, T. (ed.), *Report from Japan Service Productivity & Innovation for Growth*, pp. 1–47. (In Japanese.)

Japan Productivity Center (2017). Comparison of service quality between Japan and the United States, in Fukao, K. (ed.), *Productivity Research Center Report*, pp. 1–48. (In Japanese.)

Juran, J.M. (1951). *Quality Control Handbook*, 1st edition. New York: McGraw-Hill.

Kajiwara, T. (2008). *Management Accounting for Quality Costs*, Tokyo: Chuokeizai-sha. (In Japanese.)

Kondo, D. (2017). Target costing for restaurant services: Consideration of the restaurant division in the Budoonoki Co., Ltd., *Melco Journal of Management Accounting Research*, Vol. 9, No. 2, pp. 35–44. (In Japanese.)

Kotler, P. and Armstrong, G. (1989). *Principles of Marketing*, 4th edition. New Jersey: Prentice Hall.

Ku, H.H., Kuo, C.C. *et al.* (2013). Is maximum customer service always a good thing? Customer satisfaction in response to over-attentive service, *Managing Service Quality: An International Journal*, Vol. 23, No. 5, pp. 437–452.

Lovelock, C. (1983). Classifying services to gain strategic marketing insights, *Journal of Marketing*, Vol. 47, No. 3, pp. 9–20.

Monden, Y. (1991). *Cost Management for Automobile Companies*. Tokyo: Dobunkan. (In Japanese.)

Nakahata, S. (2013). Listen to customers and "co-create" services that benefits the society, *New Top*, Vol. 43, pp. 15–17. (In Japanese.)

Nakahata, S. (2016). Work illustrations: For customer satisfaction, *JA-kyosai*, Vol. 11, pp. 18–21. (In Japanese.)

Okada, Y. (2007). Theoretical consideration of service target costing: A focus on service management theory, *Frontier of Japanese Corporate Research*, Vol. 3, pp. 107–126. (In Japanese.)

Okamoto, K. (2000). *Cost Accounting*, 6th edition. Tokyo: Kunimoto Syobo Co., Ltd. (In Japanese.)

Oliver, R. (1980). A cognitive model of the antecedents and consequences of satisfaction decisions, *Journal of Marketing Research*, Vol. 17, No. 4, pp. 460–469.

Oliver, R.L., Rust, R.T. *et al.* (1997). Customer delight: Foundations, findings, and managerial insight, *Journal of Retailing*, Vol. 73, No. 3, pp. 311–336.

Parasuraman, A., Zeithaml, V.A. *et al.* (1988). SERQUAL: A multiple-item scale for measuring consumer perceptions of service quality, *Journal of Retailing*, Vol. 64, No. 1, pp. 12–40.

Shimada, Y. (2010). Efforts for leveling in the laundry industry, *IE Review*, Vol. 51, No. 2, pp. 11–16. (In Japanese.)

Shimada, Y. (2015). Realization of operation leveling and customer expansion, *Service Process Improvement Casebook*. Tokyo: Service Productivity & Innovation for Growth. (In Japanese.)

Tanimori, M. and Tasaka, K. (2013). Case study of the application of target costing in bank: Progress of target costing in the service industry, *Financial and Cost Accounting*, Vol. 73, No. 3, pp. 66–76. (In Japanese.)

Wang, Z. (2009). Quality control as a means of cost management, *Hitotsubashi Review of Commerce and Management*, Vol. 4, No. 2, pp. 37–48. (In Japanese.)

Zeithaml, V.A., Parasuraman, A. *et al*. (1985). Problems and strategies in services marketing, *Journal of Marketing*, Vol. 49, No. 2, pp. 33–46.

Chapter 10

Evaluation Method of Return on Equity

Tohru Furuyama

Kaetsu University, Tokyo 187-8578, Japan
t-furuyama@kaetsu.ac.jp

This study seeks to examine the necessary conditions to raise Japanese companies' return on equity (ROE), which has been under the effect of a declining trend since the 1980s. Thus, I determine which evaluation method would be most suitable for this purpose. In general, ROE is decomposed and evaluated by the DuPont model. However, this model does not accurately measure the contribution of leverage in ROE, leading to an incorrect evaluation. In this paper, I investigated the differences between the DuPont and the Moriwaki models. The results show that there are significant differences in the perception of leverage effects. We can say that the Moriwaki model is a more appropriate model to recognize the contribution of leverage effect to ROE.

1. Introduction

In this study, I analyze the Moriwaki (2002) model of assessing return on equity (ROE), first proposed by noted economist Akira Moriwaki. A time-series analysis of Japanese companies' ROE using this model reveals that lower leverage and falling assets turnover are the cause of Japan's long-term ROE decline.

Ever since the report published by Ito (2014), the declining ROE of Japanese companies has been a topic of intense discussion. One problem held responsible for this trend is low profit margins. However, in this study, I identify a different problem.

Despite the difference between time-series and cross-sectional analyses, I examine why discrepancies particularly arise in the evaluation of ROE from the *same* Japanese company. To understand this predicament, I compare the result of the DuPont and Moriwaki models.

I use data from the Financial Statements Statistics of Corporation by Industry[1,2] to analyze the ROE of Japanese companies. Two analytical methods are used: the Moriwaki and the DuPont models. I thereafter clarify the difference between their theoretical and numerical characteristics.

2. The DuPont Model: Issues and Problems

2.1 *Ito (2014) review*

The Ito (2014) review represents the established view of Japanese companies on ROE. Ito attributes the long-term stagnation of ROE in Japanese companies to a low profit margin on sales. To elaborate, when compared internationally, the ROE of Japanese companies is low, and a systematic analysis shows there is no difference in leverage or assets turnover. What is evident, though, is the low profit margin.

Investors realize that ROE is an important ratio for measuring profitability, whereas Japanese companies view it to be the result of past economic performance than the management goal.

Thus, ROE does not aim to maximize profits, but it aims to exceed the minimum cost of capital. In fact, it is challenging to incorporate ROE as a management goal. Moreover, raising leverage is not considered a good

---

[1]There are annual and quarterly surveys of corporate statistical data, but I use data from quarterly surveys. In the annual survey, profit items have been surveyed up to net income. However, the quarterly survey deals with ordinary income, and hence ROEBT is used in lieu of ROE.

[2]Because these data are quarterly data, the seasonality cannot be excluded if the data are used as they are. Otherwise, the value calculated by the annual value is different from the order. To solve these problems, the indicators are calculated after converting them to annual data using the first to the fourth quarter.

method because it involves increased risk. These two reasons are primarily why ROE is not considered important. It is also pointed out that the awareness of capital costs, which are important for evaluating ROE, is low internationally.

2.2 *Literature on ROE evaluation*

In this study, I examine three articles published in the June 2015 special issue of the *Security Analysts Journal*: "ROE Improvement to Increase Corporate Value." These articles were authored by Kobayashi (2015), on governance in capital productivity; Yanagi (2015), who responds to the Ito review; and Miyagawa (2015), who analyzed the low ROE of Japanese companies with 1x Price Book Ratio (PBR) asymmetry.[3]

Kobayashi (2015) views ROE as a proxy variable for total factor productivity. After decomposing ROE using the DuPont model, the author argues that the low ROE in Japan can be attributed to the low profit margin on sales compared with Western companies. On the other hand, the total assets turnover and leverage are not markedly different.

Yanagi (2015) states that the cost of capital is important for evaluating ROE, with emphasis on the equity spread. Despite improvements in Japanese ROE, it is *still* considered internationally low because of low margins. Here as well, Yanagi concludes that total assets turnover and leverage are not substantially different. The author comes to this conclusion by decomposing ROE using the DuPont model, and then comparing the results with US companies.

Miyagawa (2015) explains the low ROE problem in relation to the PBR: If the PBR is less than 1, the stock price will not rise, even if ROE exceeds the cost of capital. Analyzing the ROE of Japanese companies over time, the author states that the decline is largely due to profit margin than leverage or turnover. However, he points out that turnover and leverage *have* declined over the past 30 years, which has also affected ROE.

---

[3]In addition, Sugishita (2015) and Aoki (2013) also pointed out that the reason for the decline in ROE is the decline in margins.

In this paper, the ROE is first decomposed using a different formula from the DuPont model. The concrete form of the decomposition formula is as follows:

$$ROE = \{ROA + (ROA - I) \times (D/E)\}\,(1 - t)$$

In the above equation, numerator of ROA is the operating profit, whereas I is the ratio of interest expenses to interest bearing liability. This differs from the Moriwaki model used herein. Miyagawa also points out that the problem with ROE for Japanese companies is the profit margin. The time-series analysis of Japanese companies' ROE (described later), however, points to a decline in leverage. The difference between these two evaluations can be ascribed to the difference in the analytical methods, namely, the DuPont model and the Moriwaki model. This difference is explained in what follows.

2.2.1 *Moriwaki model: Time-series analysis of ROE*

In the Moriwaki model used herein, the ROE before tax, or ROEBT, is the analysis target ratio that allows me to eliminate the effects of taxes that are not closely related to business management. The analysis of ROEBT is illustrated in Fig. 1.

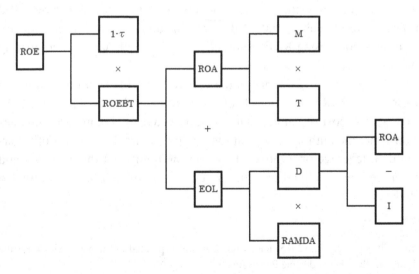

Fig. 1. Method of analysis for ROEBT in the Moriwaki model.

Source: Moriwaki (2002).

The calculation formula for each ratio is as follows:

ROEBT (tax – included basis) (%)
= Profit before tax/ Total net assets
(Average at the beginning and end of period) × 100

ROA (%)
= Income before income taxes ÷ total assets
(average at beginning and end of period) × 100

However,

Income before income taxes = Finance costs + Income before
income taxes

M(%) [Net income before income taxes before income taxes]
= Net income before income taxes before income taxes /
Sales × 100

T(*times/year*) [total asset turnover]
= Sales / total assets
(average at the beginning and end of the period)

I(%) [debt interest rate]
= finance costs / (total assets
(average at the beginning of the period)
– net assets (average at the end of the period)) × 100

RAMDA (times) [debt equity ratio]
= (total assets (average at the beginning of the period) –
net assets (average at the end of the period)) ÷
total net assets (average at the end of the period)

D (%) [difference] = ROA – I

EOL (%) [efficiency of liabilities] = D × RAMDA

Here, the total assets are the average at the beginning and at the end of the fiscal year, including the discounted notes receivable and transferred endorsed notes.

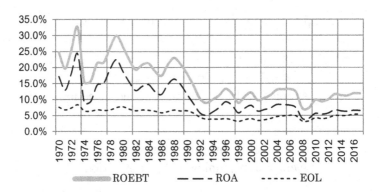

Fig. 2.   Trend of ROEBT, ROA, and EOL of Japanese companies.

Source: Data: Financial Statements Statistics of Corporations by Industry.

I calculate each ratio in the Moriwaki model using data collected from the Financial Statements Statistics of Corporations by Industry and analyze the fluctuation factors of the ROEBT of Japanese companies (hereinafter, "ROE").[4] Specifically, among other values, I calculate the ROE, return on assets (ROA), and effect of leverage (EOL) used in the Moriwaki model using the above dataset. I thus show the transition of these indicators. Figure 2 illustrates the changes in ROE, ROA, and EOL, whereas Fig. 3 illustrates the breakdown of ROE into ROA and EOL. Figure 4 illustrates the breakdown of ROE differences by calculating the difference from the previous period of ROE, ROA, and EOL.

As Fig. 3 shows, the cause of the decline in ROE is mostly due to the decline in EOL.

As Fig. 4 shows, changes in ROE are very strongly influenced by EOL. Figures 2–4 thus confirm that the decline in ROE of Japanese companies is due to the decline in EOL.

In Fig. 5, EOL is broken down into difference (D) and debt ratio (RAMDA). I find that, from the 1970s to the 1980s, EOL was exceptionally high, between 15% and 20%, against the backdrop of high D and high

---

[4] The data of the corporate quarterly report have been available since 1960. However, because the value at the beginning and end of the balance sheet items is available from 1969 only, the data from 1970 to 2018 are used to calculate the ratio. The income statement item uses the total value from the second to the first quarter of the following year as the value for that year.

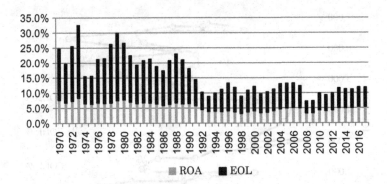

Fig. 3.   Trend of ROA and EOL for Japanese companies.
Source: Data: Financial Statements Statistics of Corporations by Industry.

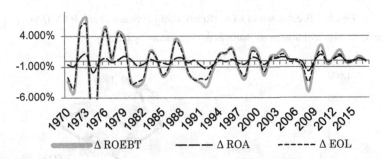

Fig. 4.   Trend of changes in ROEBT, ROA, and EOL for Japanese companies.
Source: Data: Financial Statements Statistics of Corporations by Industry.

RAMDA. In the 1990s, EOL fell to a value of 5%–10% due to a drop in D. Since then, D has risen over the 2000s, but the rise in EOL has been modest due to the decline in RAMDA. D rose further over the 2010s, surpassing the 1970s and 1980s. However, due to a decline in RAMDA, EOL remained low during this period: only 5%–10%. Thus, EOL evidently declined because of a decline in RAMDA.

Figure 6 shows ROA — the other element of ROE — split into net profit margin (M) and total assets turnover (T). Here, ROA can be divided into three periods from the M and T scenarios. In other words, the first period was from 1970 to 1980, characterized by high ROA due to high M and high T. The second period was from the 1990s to the 2000s, characterized by the lowest ROA due to a decline in M and T. The third period is

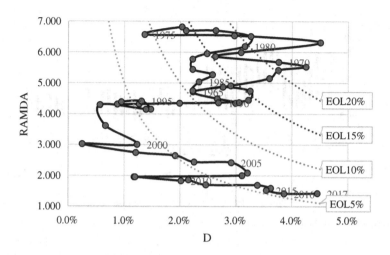

Fig. 5. Breakdown of EOL (Relationship between *D* and RAMDA).

Source: Data: Financial Statements Statistics of Corporations by Industry.

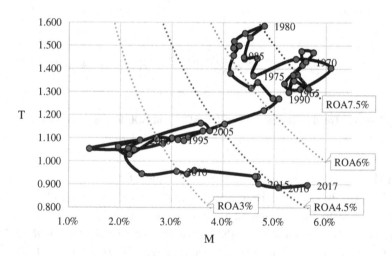

Fig. 6. Breakdown of ROA (Relationship between M and T).

Source: Data: Financial Statements Statistics of Corporations by Industry.

the 2010s, when M rose significantly, but T rose further. Consequently, ROA remained low. During this period, M rose to the same level as the highest level in the early 1970s. However, since T fell to about 70% compared with the 1970s and 1980s, ROA was only 5% during this period. Thus, the ROA of Japanese companies declined due to a decline in T.

As mentioned above, when conducting a time-series analysis of the ROE of Japanese companies using the Moriwaki model, I find that ROE declined due to a decline in EOL and RAMDA, whereas ROA, the other factor, declined due to a decline in T. As a result, it is necessary to raise RAMDA and T to raise the ROE of Japanese companies again.[5,6]

3. The DuPont and Moriwaki Models: A Comparison

Next, I compare the DuPont and the Moriwaki models. The comparison is based on both theoretical and numerical characteristics.

3.1 *Theoretical characteristics*

The DuPont model is originally expressed by the following formula:

$$ROE = M \times T \times L,$$

where ROE represents return on equity (net income/equity), M represents net profit margin (net income/sales), T represents total assets turnover (sales/total assets), and L represents financial leverage (total assets/equity).

To distinguish from the ratio of the Moriwaki model, I denote M in the DuPont model as M_D, T as T_D, and L as L_D. However, in the corporate statistics quarterly report's corporate profit data, the recurring profit is used as the company profit. As a result, the equation of ROE is the recurring profit divided by the equity in this study.

Then, the Moriwaki model is expressed by the following formula:

$$ROEBT = ROA + EOL$$
$$= ROA + D \times RAMDA$$
$$= ROA + (ROA - I) \times RAMDA$$

---

[5]In Furuyama (1994), Furuyama (2008a), and Furuyama (2008b), it was pointed out that EOL has a very high explanatory power for ROE and that the decline in EOL is due to the decline in RAMDA.

[6]Kojima and Fujiwara (2016) show a long-term decline in the debt ratio (RAMDA) of Japanese firms, noting that in recent years, the debt ratio has stopped falling and, conversely, has been rising.

This model uses the recurring profit as the numerator of ROE (ROEBT). In the discussion herein, I compare only the right-hand side of the model formula.

There are two major differences between the DuPont and the Moriwaki models: (1) Leverage handling and (2) the ROA concept. I now reconfirm these differences.

First, consider the difference in the handling of leverage. The leverage of the DuPont model represented by L_D affects the entire equation. On the other hand, the leverage of the Moriwaki model represented by RAMDA affects only the second term. The DuPont model claims that L_D should be raised to increase the ROE on the left-hand side. As long as M_D, which can take a negative value, is positive, ROE can be raised by increasing L_D. The Moriwaki model argues that ROE can be raised by increasing RAMDA if the value shown by D is positive. If D is negative, increasing RAMDA will lead to lower ROE (Table 1).

The Moriwaki model considers the flow of money from equity and debt. It particularly focuses on this point. That is, it shows the performance of money flow from equity to be the first term on the right-hand side and the performance of money flow from debt as the second term on the right-hand side.

In the DuPont model, ROE is a monomial expression expressed as a product of three variables, whereas, in the Moriwaki model, ROE is expressed as the sum of two terms: ROA (profitability) and EOL (leverage effect). Thus, the Moriwaki model allows us to understand the relationship between ROE and its components with ease. In other words, it can grasp the degree to which ROE contributes to profitability and the leverage effect, whereas the DuPont model cannot. If the change from

Table 1.   Concept of ROE analysis in the Moriwaki model.

Contribution to ROE	Net return	Total return		Balance sheet		Cost
EOL = D × RAMDA	D = ROA2 − I	ROA2	ROA	Total assets	Liabilities	I
ROA = ROA1 × 1	ROA1 − 0	ROA1			Equity	Zero

Note: "I" is the ratio of interest on liabilities; ROA1 = ROA2.

the previous quarter is considered, the Moriwaki model can still clearly grasp profitability and the leverage effect. Again, the DuPont model fails here.

Because the DuPont model shows ROE as a product of three elements, the higher the three elements, the higher the ROE; and the higher the profit margin on sales and the total assets turnover ratio, the more the positive effect on ROE. Though this seems logical, in the case of financial leverage, the higher the ratio, the higher the risk. Therefore, it is difficult to explain how the positive effect on ROE will increase as the ratio increases. On the other hand, in the Moriwaki model, RAMDA (debt ratio) corresponding to the financial leverage of the DuPont model is included only in EOL, which is the second term. Hence, it only affects EOL. Here, it can be seen that the capital structure is an important factor in determining whether the leverage effect is easily understood. Moreover, the other element of EOL is D (= ROA-I), and only when this is positive, RAMDA acts to raise ROE. When D is negative, RAMDA lowers ROE. This reasoning is intuitive.

Second, there is a difference in the concept of ROA. The ROA in the DuPont model is M_D × T_D. It is obtained by dividing profit by total assets, making it a type of ROA. However, the numerator is the profit-after-interest payment, which is different from ROA.

In the Moriwaki model, the first term on the right-hand side is a ratio with the before-interest payment profit over the total assets. That is, ROA is included in the model formula. ROA is also an element of *item 2*; it shows relative profitability compared with the interest burden. This is consistent with the business process, and it is intuitive.

When viewed in relation to business decision-making, ROA and EOL are different functions. In other words, ROA, which is the product of margin (M) and assets turnover (T), is a ratio that easily underscores a deep relationship with production and sales activities. However, EOL is a ratio that makes it challenging to assume the relationship with actual production and sales activities. This is because EOL is an indicator that should be controlled in management, which is a higher-level concept, rather than in the business field.

Thus, improving production and sales activities can increase profit margins or speed up assets turnover. However, D, which is the difference between ROA and the total procurement cost, and leverage, which should be determined based on such margins, are not verified solely based on the production and sales activities. Therefore, both ROA and EOL decision-making should be separate and, thus, the two should be understood separately as well. The Moriwaki model is a system that enables such measurements, but the DuPont model does not take this point into consideration.

3.2 *Numerical characteristics*

Next, I compare the two models in terms of numerical values. Specifically, I calculate the analytical indices of the two models using the data of the Financial Statements Statistics of Corporations by Industry, calculate the contribution of each analytical ratio, and compare the two models.

The data used for the calculation are for all industries in all scales of the Financial Statements Statistics of Corporations by Industry. Using these data, I calculate the ROE and the analytical indicators of the two models from Financial Year (FY) 1970 to FY 2017 as well as the contribution of the analytical indicators for each fiscal year. I then evaluate the two models using the average value for all years compared.

The data of the Financial Statements Statistics of Corporations by Industry have been available since the first quarter of 1960. However, there are limitations to using these data as published. I thus convert them into data for one year by integrating the data of four quarters. The balance sheet figures are averaged over the year. The figures on income statements are the sum of the values within the fiscal year. The data of the balance sheet in the Financial Statements Statistics of Corporations by Industry include data at the beginning and at the end of the term. However, because these data are available only from 1969 onward, I use the data from 1970 to 2017 to calculate the indicators.

Table 2 reports the results from calculating the value of the analysis ratio using the data of the corporate statistical quarterly from 1970 to 2017, the contribution of the analysis ratio for each fiscal year, and the average and median values.

First, I find that the contribution to a change in ROE is higher in EOL than in ROA in the Moriwaki model. The contribution to a change in EOL

Table 2. Comparison from FY1970 to FY2017.

Analysis by Moriwaki model	Average	Median
ΔROE		
Contribution of ROA	17.949%	19.299%
Contribution of EOL	**82.051%**	**80.701%**
ΔROA		
Contribution of M	**75.206%**	**94.852%**
Contribution of T	24.780%	7.101%
Contribution of M&T	−0.420%	−1.953%
ΔEOL		
Contribution of D	**103.073%**	**78.402%**
Contribution of RAMDA	−5.144%	23.103%
Contribution of D&RAMDA	−3.054%	−1.505%
ΔD		
Contribution of ROA	**88.477%**	**87.460%**
Contribution of I	11.523%	12.540%
Analysis by Dupont model	**Average**	**Median**
ΔROE		
Contribution of ROA_D	**105.808%**	**109.667%**
Contribution of L_D	−5.643%	−4.908%
Contribution of ROA_D&L_D	−2.269%	−4.759%
ΔROA_DP		
Contribution of M_D	**89.530%**	**169.447%**
Contribution of T_D	10.007%	−65.273%
Contribution of M_D&T_D	−0.802%	−4.174%

Source: Data: Financial Statements Statistics of Corporations by Industry.

is higher in D than in RAMDA. The contribution to a change in D is higher in ROA than in I. Finally, the contribution to a change in ROA is higher for M than for T. When it is divided into ROA and EOL, the contribution of EOL is high. However, further examination shows that ROA has a higher contribution, whereas M contributes greatly to ROA.

On the other hand, for the DuPont model, ROA_D contributes more to ROE changes than L_D does and M_D contributes more to ROA_D changes than T_D does. That is, M significantly contributes to ROE.

4. Conclusion

In this paper, I calculated the ROE using the data of the Financial Statements Statistics of Corporations by Industry and compared the evaluation of the Moriwaki and the DuPont models. My analysis confirms that the net profit margin (M or M_D) has a substantial effect on ROE, as already established.

However, the results from both analyses were markedly different regarding whether the effect of margin can be recognized as part of the leverage effect. In this respect, the Moriwaki model confirms that the M or ROA effect contributes to ROE by dividing it into two paths: the direct effect and the indirect effect of the leverage effect. In the DuPont model, the direct and indirect effects cannot be grasped separately.

Both the models show that the margin indicator has the strongest effect on ROE. Strictly speaking, there is a difference between the DuPont model with profit-after-interest payments and the Moriwaki model with profit-before-interest payments as the numerator. However, the conclusion remains the same, the difference being in terms of how ROE could be increased. The Moriwaki model shows that it is necessary to raise the profit margin and leverage effect, whereas the DuPont model only accepts the former condition. Both models show that the margin indicator has the strongest effect on ROE.

However, the conclusions from the two models differed regarding the conditions necessary to raise the ROE. In other words, the Moriwaki model showed that it is necessary to raise the profit margin and leverage effect, whereas the DuPont model could not confirm this point.

We know that the difference between the two models rests heavily on whether the leverage effect is considered an independent element. The ROA comprising M and T can be raised by improving the efficiency of the company's business cycle. However, I and RAMDA — elements of EOL — are determined by factors that have no relation to the efficiency of a company's business cycle, that is, management judgment. In other words, if the premise were that the indicator is based on the actual ROA, the path to achieving the target ROE value includes an element determined by the management decision, called EOL.

In this case, the management recognizes the degree of difference (D) between ROA and the borrowing cost and, thus, determines the debt ratio (RAMDA). This way, the target ROE is achieved, and ROE is thus controlled. For this purpose, ROA and EOL need to be measured separately by using the Moriwaki model, which can recognize the leverage effect of EOL. Thus, an appropriate management decision can be made, and the target ROE can be determined.

In this chapter, I analyzed the data of the Financial Statements Statistics of Corporations by Industry while considering the availability and handling of the data. However, this source contains data of unaudited small and medium-size enterprises, leading to an issue of reliability, a limitation I would like to address in future by using public company data for further analyses.

References

Aoki, S. (2013). Profitability of Japanese, American and European companies (manufacturing), *Journal of Ibaraki Christian College. I, Humanities, II, Social and Natural Sciences*, Vol. 47, pp. 143–151.

Furuyama, T. (1994). *Features of ROE by Industry*, Business Analysis Research Annual Report No. 10, pp. 102–107, Business Analysis Association.

Furuyama, T. (2008a). *Characteristics of Profitability Structures by Industry*, Japan Society for Management Education Research Report, Japan Association for Management Education.

Furuyama, T. (2008b). *Study on Performance Evaluation Indicators of Banking Business*, pp. 61–70, The Small and Medium-sized Companies and Venture Business Consortium of Japan.

Ito, K. (2014). Ito Review of Competitiveness and Incentives for Sustainable Growth — Building Favorable Relationships between Companies and Investors — Final Report. https://www.meti.go.jp/english/policy/economy/corporate_governance/pdf/FRIR.pdf.

Kobayashi, K. (2015). The era of capital productivity: From bank governance to equity governance, *Secur. Anal. J.*, Vol. 53, No. 6, pp. 6–16.

Kojima, H. and Fujiwara, S. (2016). *Recent Balance Sheet Adjustment of Japanese Companies: Evaluation from the Theory of Optimal Capital Structure*, Bank of Japan Review. https://www.boj.or.jp/research/wps_rev/rev_2016/rev16j14.htm/.

Miyagawa, K. (2015). Low-ROE problem of Japanese companies that appear to be 1 × asymmetry of PBR, *Secur. Anal. J.*, Vol. 53, No. 6, pp. 28–38.

Moriwaki, S. (2002). *How to Use Financial Statements for Stable Management of Companies*, Taxation Research Institute Publishing Bureau. ISBN: 4793111858, 978-4793111853.

Sugishita, H. (2015). Dividend return policy for sustainable ROE and improvement of shareholder value, *Secur. Anal. J.*, Vol. 53, No. 6, pp. 39–48.

Yanagi, R. (2015). The desirable relationship between companies and investors for improving ROE: In response to Ito report, *Secur. Anal. J.*, Vol. 53, No. 6, pp. 17–27.

Chapter 11

Strategic Investment Decision Processes in Semiconductor Production Equipment Companies

Soichiro Higashi

Postdoctoral Researcher, Graduate School of Business Administration,
Kwansei Gakuin University,
Hyogo 662-8501, Japan

1. Introduction

The semiconductor market periodically repeats alternating waves of depression and the advent of innovative new products, called the silicon cycle. According to the IC Guidebook, this market pattern has existed since 1970, for more than 40 years, and continues today. Consequently, capital investment by semiconductor production equipment companies is surrounded by uncertainty about whether technological innovation in miniaturization and integration will continue in the future. Since the capital expenditures of semiconductor companies drive the sales of semiconductor production equipment companies, it is important that capital investment decisions by semiconductor production equipment companies consider the state of capital investment by their customers, the semiconductor companies.

In this study, I develop a reconstructed regression analysis model of capital investment in semiconductor companies and semiconductor production equipment companies. The case of Company A, a semiconductor production equipment company, is used to clarify the strategic investment

165

management process, which is thought to be directly related to the sustainability of semiconductor production equipment companies.

2. Review of Prior Research and Research Design

2.1 *Prior research on capital investment decision-making*

Prior research on capital budgets (capital investment budgets) has been based on two perspectives: economic valuation techniques and capital budgets as a management process (Shimizu *et al.*, 2010). Research on economic valuation techniques has examined why the collection period method is frequently used, while a well-known technique, discounted cash flows, is rarely used in practice, and how economic valuation techniques influence financial performance. However, research on capital budgeting as a management process is extremely limited (Shimizu *et al.*, 2010). Prior research on capital budgeting as a management process is summarized as follows.

Yamamoto (1998), a study that focuses on the capital budget management process in Japan, describes investment processes and strategic investment decisions using questionnaires and interviews with members of the manufacturing industry. In the economic evaluation technique for equipment investment, in addition to whether the calculation is reasonable, Yamamoto (1998) points out that equipment investment decisions are complementary to other measures, such as management processes and organizational soundness, and presents a framework for strategic investment decisions. Yamamoto (2008) also considers capital investment decisions from an organizational point of view. It is pointed out that to achieve objectives with limited reasonableness, accounting information provided by the accounting system is used to control organizational behavior.

Sugiyama (2002) points out the lack of a strategic perspective in traditional capital budgeting. Companies incorporate strategic thinking into their analyses to obtain a sustainable competitive advantage and make investment decisions focused on achieving the most favorable cash flow possible. In particular, for purposes of investments such as those for advanced manufacturing technology and IT investment, we do not rely solely on narrowly-defined financial indicators such as net present value and internal rate of return. Rather, Sugiyama (2002) suggests exploring an approach that appropriately considers strategic perspectives and intangible benefits.

Kato and Yamamoto (2012) point out that companies cannot risk the capital investment decision process resulting in investments that are irrelevant to a company's future strategy. There are many factors that are not taken into account in economic calculations, and a thorough evaluation is required. Therefore, it is not necessary for firms to follow along with industry practices, although capital investment decisions should respect the results of capital investment economic calculations. Rather, it has been pointed out that it is natural for companies to use different processes to make decisions.

Asada (2017) also pointed out that investment project selection is the result of various management factors, where the plan that seems to be the best one overall is the one selected. In investment projects, economic factors as well as strategic and technical priorities are emphasized more than profitability priorities. These studies point out that the capital investment decisions implemented are complementary to corporate strategies, as well as being computationally reasonable using refined economic valuation techniques.

2.2 *Research design*

The traditional management accounting concept of capital budgeting is to refine economic evaluation techniques, make calculation more reasonable, and eliminate uncertainty related to equipment investments, with the result being more reliable decision-making. The problem with economic valuation techniques is that an investment's future cash inflows are always estimated and there are always alternative estimates that could be chosen.

In the semiconductor industry, as technological innovation continues, corporate actions to continuously make capital investments are considered essential. When making a capital investment decision in the semiconductor production equipment company where I worked (Company A), it was difficult to estimate the future cash inflows of capital investments with technological innovation, as we did not know what technological innovations would occur. Even if we were able to estimate future cash inflows, the estimates were extremely inaccurate. Moreover, there are not always two or more capital investment alternatives, and without alternatives, decisions are made without applying economic valuation techniques. To continuously realize the technological innovation represented by miniaturization and integration, capital investment decisions by semiconductor production equipment companies (such as Company A) are closely related to strategic investment decisions. Thus, the pursuit of computational reasonableness and the use of refined economic evaluation techniques represent only part of the investment decision process.

Since the capital investments of semiconductor companies are the sales of semiconductor production equipment companies, it is extremely important for semiconductor production equipment companies to consider the capital investment environment of semiconductor companies when making their own capital investment decisions. Therefore, it is important not to consider the capital investments of semiconductor companies and those of semiconductor production equipment companies separately, but to consider the mutual relationship between the two. This research clarifies the process of strategic investment decision-making in semiconductor production equipment companies that are considered deeply involved in corporate strategies. My practical experience in the capital investment decision-making process in the semiconductor production equipment company (Company A) is used as an example. Based on the case, a restructured capital investment regression analysis model for semiconductor companies and semiconductor production equipment companies is added as a new perspective, and a method of making strategic investment decisions in semiconductor production equipment companies is proposed.

3. Decision-Making Uncertainty in Organization

Yamamoto (2008) describes organization decision-making styles using the uncertainty of cause and effect relationships involved in decision-making and its consequences, and the uncertainty of objectives shared by multiple decision makers, Each is categorized based on high and low levels. The study points out that the functions of accounting systems that

Table 1.   Style of decision-making and accounting system functions.

	Uncertainty of objectives			
	Low	High		
Style of decision making	Decision by computation	Decision by compromise	Low	Uncertainty of cause and effect relationships
	Answer machines	Ammunition machines		
Functions of accounting systems	Decision by judgement	Decision by judgment	High	
	Learning machines	Rationalization machines		

Source: Yamamoto (2008, p. 163. Chart 5-1 and p. 169, Chart 5-2).

Table 2.   Functions of accounting systems in practice.

	Uncertainty of objectives			
	Low	High		
Functions of accounting systems in practice	Answer machines	Persuasion machines	Low	Uncertainty of cause and effect relationships
		Justification machines	High	

Source: Yamamoto (2008, p. 163, Chart 5-3).

provide accounting information that is effective for decision-making differ because the level of uncertainty varies depending on an organization's decision-making situation (Table 1). Using an all too unsatisfactory "machine" analogy, Tables 1 and 2 outline a set of organizational roles that might help us appreciate some of the ways accounting systems function in practice (Earl and Hopwood, 1979; Burchell *et al.*, 1980).

When the cause and effect relationships and objectives both have low uncertainty, the accounting information required for organizational decision-making is the optimal solution, so "decision by computation" is the appropriate method. This points out that, in this situation, calculations using economic evaluation techniques are the best solution for capital budgeting (Yamamoto, 2008, pp. 168–169). On the other hand, when cause and effect relationships and objectives are highly uncertain, the only way to make a "decision by inspiration" using accounting information is if the accounting information provided triggers the decision maker's creativity. We expect the accounting system to provide useful accounting information that can be used to depict decision-making (Yamamoto, 2008,

p. 172). This situation suggests that calculations using economic valuation techniques cannot be used alone to make capital budgeting decisions.

With the increase in size and complexity of corporate organizations in recent years, there has been a demand for formulation and objectification of knowledge in business management. For this reason, decision-making in companies has advanced to programmed economic evaluation techniques and procedures. As a result, accounting information is used instinctively, and the actual function of the accounting system (Table 2) is different from that shown in Table 1.

In actual organizational decision-making, reasonable accounting calculation information is provided by the accounting system regardless of the degree of uncertainty of cause and effect relationships and organizational goals. The accounting system is used as a means of ex-post justification of decisions already made, even in the case of a "decision by inspiration," in which both cause and effect relationships and objectives are highly uncertain (Yamamoto, 2008, pp. 173–182).

Thus, decision-making in an organization is controlled based on the accounting information provided by the accounting system. For this reason, it is possible to consider the necessity of constructing a means of providing useful accounting information even for a "decision by inspiration."

4. Semiconductor Production Equipment Company Example (Company A)

Capital investments by semiconductor production equipment companies are greatly influenced by the trend of semiconductor company capital investment plans. Unlike semiconductor companies, capital investments of semiconductor production equipment companies are not related to construction of a production line, but many of them are producing the equivalent of prototypes of semiconductor production equipment sold to semiconductor companies. After purchasing semiconductor production equipment, semiconductor companies incorporate the equipment into their production lines, which cannot be stopped without a great deal of trouble. Therefore, it is necessary for semiconductor production equipment companies to reproduce the problems experienced in semiconductor companies and establish a method for solving them using the equivalent of the semiconductor production equipment sold to those companies.

The budget for annual capital investment (hereinafter referred to as the "capital budget") at Company A is formulated in accordance with the initial plan and the medium-term management plan. Based on the capital investment plans of semiconductor companies (which is equivalent to the semiconductor production equipment company's sales plan), capital investment projects are accumulated, formulated, and selected. At the time the plan is developed, the company may not have decided whether to use the economic evaluation techniques for specific equipment investments, so the decision differs depending on the person in charge. Although this is highly uncertain at the time the capital budget is prepared, capital investment and future cash inflow are predicted. In fact, Company A adopts the recovery period method, which is one of the economic evaluation techniques used for capital investments. When an annual capital budget is determined, the cap on total investment in one accounting period is fixed and the investment project is selected.

In general, investments in capital budgets are roughly classified into two types: strategic investments (investments in new products, investments in advanced manufacturing technologies, mergers and acquisitions of companies, etc.) and business investments (replacement investments, investments for expanding existing facilities, investments in products/markets similar to existing businesses, etc.) (Sugiyama, 2008). Company A finds the latest technologies, such as miniaturization, integration, and wafer size, changes the platform of equipment (useful life, 3 to 10 years), and invests in versatile equipment as a strategic investment. This cutting-edge technology investment is directly linked to the company's sustainability. Therefore, it is necessary to continuously carry out capital investments based on the plan at the time the capital budget is selected. On the other hand, it is difficult to estimate the future cash inflows of cutting-edge technology investments. Even if estimates can be made, their accuracy is extremely low, making it impossible to make a decision using only economic evaluation techniques. For this reason, strategic investments of semiconductor production equipment companies are considered to fall under "decision by inspiration," where, as noted in the previous section, the causal relationships and objectives are highly uncertain. Thus, the semiconductor capital investment model is reconstructed to provide accounting information that is useful for decision-making.

5. Reconstruction of Semiconductor Capital Investment Model

5.1 *Outline of semiconductor capital investment model*

Based on Higashi's (2017) capital investment model of semiconductor companies and semiconductor production equipment companies, where the dependent variable is capital investment, and the independent variables are cash flow, debt ratio, and the book-to-bill (BB) ratio, regression analysis was performed again for the period from fiscal 1999 to fiscal 2016, which extended the 1999–2014 period by two years. "Cash flow" and "debt ratio" are calculated based on the Nikkei NEEDS-Financial QUEST. "BB ratio" is calculated based on Cabinet Office Economic and Social Research Institute, (2001–2008), Cabinet Office, (2009–2017) and the Nikkei NEEDS-Financial QUEST.

5.2 *Overview of BB ratio*

The BB ratio is a leading indicator of supply and demand in the semiconductor market. This is the ratio of the order value (booking) to the shipment value (billing). Since the order value corresponds to demand and the shipment value (sales) corresponds to supply, the ratio indicates the balance between supply and demand. If the BB ratio is higher than 1.0, demand is strong and future shipments will increase, indicating that the industry's business sentiment and market conditions are strong. On the other hand, if it is below 1.0, the future shipment value will decrease due to oversupply, indicating the industry's business sentiment and market conditions are sluggish. Monthly orders and shipments use a BB ratio averaged over the last three months to compensate for irregular fluctuations caused by semiconductor companies' speculative purchases. If the order and shipment (sales) amounts are in balance, the BB ratio equals 1.0, indicating a balance between supply and demand. According to newspaper articles on Nikkei Inc., as a guideline, the BB ratio during a steady demand expansion period is said to be 1.2 to 1.3 and in the demand expansion period is said to be about 1.05 to 1.10.

Since semiconductors are electronic components that were initially developed and produced in the United States, the semiconductor market originated primarily in the United States. In 1978, the Semiconductor Industry Association (SIA) began to announce the semiconductor BB ratios in the North American region, and as a result, the ratio gained worldwide attention as an indicator of the silicon cycle or the wave of semiconductor supply and demand. However, as globalization has increased, semiconductor production has spread to regions other than North America, such as Asia, and North America is no longer representative of the world's semiconductor supply and demand situation. SIA stopped releasing the BB ratio after December 1996.

Currently, semiconductor companies place orders for semiconductor production equipment prior to semiconductor production, so the BB ratio of semiconductor production equipment has come to be used as a leading indicator for the entire industry. In the United States, the semiconductor production equipment company headquarters in North America, the BB ratio is announced monthly by Semiconductor Equipment and Materials International (SEMI). In Japan, the BB ratio of Japanese semiconductor production equipment is announced monthly by the Semiconductor Equipment Association of Japan (SEAJ), an industry group.

5.3 *Regression analysis of the semiconductor capital investment model*

The target companies are semiconductor companies and semiconductor production equipment companies that existed from fiscal 1999 to fiscal 2016, and whose consolidated financial statements can be viewed from the Nikkei NEEDS-Financial QUEST. For semiconductor companies, the semiconductor industry planning overview of capital investments by 30 companies from 1999 to 2016 was used to select 13 semiconductor companies that meet these conditions; nine semiconductor production equipment companies were also selected. Based on Higashi's (2016a, 2016b, 2017) results, each independent variable is lagged by one year for semiconductor companies and by two years for semiconductor production equipment companies compared to the capital investment amount, which is the dependent variable. The regression analysis with the highest degrees of freedom adjusted determination coefficient (adjR^2) was selected (Table 3).

Table 3.   Regression analysis results of the semiconductor capital investment model.

Target period	Independent variables	OCF	DR	BB	b_0	adjR^2
(a) Capital investment model of semiconductor companies						
1999–2016	Rug		−1	−1		
	VIF	1.05	1.14	1.10		
	B	4.34	−14.92	91.87	−21.35	0.606
	β	0.13	−0.35	0.64		
	t value	0.83	−2.10	3.87	−0.54	
	p value	0.42	0.06	0.00	0.60	
(b) Capital investment model of semiconductor production equipment companies						
1999–2016	Rug	−2	−2	−2		
	VIF	1.69	1.77	1.31		
	B	7.17	−3.86	7.49	5.55	0.655
	β	0.28	−0.58	0.49		
	t value	1.44	−2.88	2.80	2.13	
	p value	0.17	0.01	0.02	0.05	

Source: Table 3 was created by the author based on Machinery Orders, Nikkei NEEDS-Financial QUEST, and Semiconductor Industry Planning Guide.

5.4 *Semiconductor capital investment model*

Capital investment model of semiconductor companies

$$I_{it} = \Delta 21.35 + 4.34 OCF_{it} - 14.92 DR_{it-1} + 91.87 BB_{t-1}$$

adjR^2 = 0.606

Capital investment model of semiconductor production equipment companies

$$I_{it} = 5.55 + 7.17 OCF_{it-2} - 3.86 DR_{it-2} + 7.49 BB_{t-2}$$

adjR^2 = 0.655

I_{it} : The amount of capital investment of company i in period t
OCF_{it} : Cash flow of company i in period t (consolidated operating cash flow)
DR_{it} : Debt ratio of company i in period t (debt ÷ equity)
BB_t : BB Ratio in period t (machinery orders)

The adjR^2 of the semiconductor company and semiconductor production equipment company capital investment model exceeds the general judgment standard of adjR^2 > 0.5, suggesting a certain level of prediction accuracy is present. As a result, the restructuring of the semiconductor capital investment model is considered to contribute to predicting capital investment amounts by combining strategic and business investment in the capital budget.

6. Conclusion

The sales of semiconductor production equipment companies are directly linked to the capital investments of semiconductor companies. Consequently, it is considered essential for semiconductor production equipment companies to always keep an eye on trends in the latest technologies, such as miniaturization, integration, and wafer size generation renewal, requested by semiconductor companies. Therefore, based on the case of Company A, the contribution of this research is that the capital investment process in semiconductor production equipment companies was clarified and the following three points were identified.

1. Strategic investment in semiconductor production equipment companies is considered "decision by inspiration," where there is high uncertainty with regard to cause and effect relationships and objectives, as noted in Section 3. This clarifies the need to establish a means of providing decision makers with useful accounting information. To accomplish this, the semiconductor capital investment model was restructured.

2. The capital investments of semiconductor production equipment companies are dependent on the trend in capital investments of semiconductor companies. Therefore, it is important not to evaluate capital

investments of semiconductor companies and those of semiconductor production equipment companies individually, but to confirm the mutual relationship between the two. This study points out that it is possible to provide useful accounting information when planning capital budgets of semiconductor production equipment companies because it is possible to foresee both capital investment amounts using the restructured semiconductor capital investment model.

3. Anticipating the amount of capital investment using the reconstructed semiconductor capital investment model also presents an economic evaluation that recognizes the capital budgets of semiconductor production equipment companies. Therefore, it contributes to reducing over — and under-investment, especially for investments in cutting-edge technologies that are strategic investments directly linked to the sustainability of semiconductor production equipment companies.

A research issue in this area, beginning in fiscal 2017, is the difficulty calculating the BB ratio, an independent variable in the semiconductor capital investment model that has been reconstructed. Some semiconductor production equipment companies have canceled the disclosure of orders since the first quarter of 2017 (April–June) to avoid large-scale short-term stock price movements based on the status of orders. As a result, the SEAJ no longer announces the BB ratio for semiconductor production equipment in Japan, and the Cabinet Office of Japan has abolished classifying semiconductor production equipment in machinery orders received. Since the BB ratio must be calculated based on limited company information beginning in FY 2017, I will consider its usefulness as a future research topic.

References

Asada, T. (2017). Cash flow management accounting for investment decision making, in Asada, T., Yori, M. *et al.* (eds.), *Management Accounting/Introduction: Management for Strategic Management Accounting*, 4th Edition, (pp. 183–206). Tokyo: Yuhikaku Publishing Co., Ltd. (In Japanese.)

Burchell, S., Clubb, C. *et al.* (1980). The roles of accounting in organizations and society, *Accounting, Organizations and Society*, Vol. 5, No. 1, pp. 5–27. Amsterdam: Elsevier.

Cabinet Office, (2009–2017). *Machinery Orders*, Tokyo: http://www.esri.cao. go.jp/jp/stat/juchu/juchu.html.

Cabinet Office Economic and Social Research Institute, (2001–2008). *Annual report of Machinery Orders*, Tokyo: Ministry of Finance Printing Bureau. (In Japanese.)

Earl, M. and Hopwood, A. (1979). *From Management Information to Information Management*. A paper presented to the IFIP TCR-WG8.2 Working Conference on the Information Systems Environment, Bonn.

Higashi, S. (2016a). Empirical research on capital investment of semiconductor companies — The effectiveness of financial indicator in Japanese semiconductor corporate realignment — Hyogo: Kwansei Gakuin University, *The Review of Economics and Business Management*, Vol. 43, pp. 131–146. (In Japanese.)

Higashi, S. (2016b). An empirical research on the capital investment of Japanese semiconductor manufacture equipment corporations — The effectiveness of book to bill ratio — *Kwansei Gakuin shogaku kenkyu*, Vol. 72, pp. 21–51. Hyogo: Kwansei Gakuin University (In Japanese.)

Higashi, S. (2017). An Empirical Research on Capital Investment in the Semiconductor Industry — Research on Semiconductor Companies and Semiconductor Production Equipment Companies in Japan — Doctoral dissertation from Kwansei Gakuin University. Hyogo: Kwansei Gakuin University (In Japanese.)

Kato, Y. and Yamamoto, K. (2012). Providing accounting information for capital investment, in Kato, Y. and Yamamoto, K. *Knowledge of Cost Accounting*, 2nd edition, (pp. 207–214). Tokyo: Nikkei Inc. (In Japanese.)

Recession in US Semiconductor Business. (1984, December 13). *The Nikkei Business Daily*, p. 1. Tokyo: Nikkei Inc.

Research Bureau of Economic Planning Agency. (1998–2000). *Annual Report of Machinery Orders*, Tokyo: Ministry of Finance Printing Bureau. (In Japanese.)

Sangyo Times, Inc. (1983–2017–18). *Semiconductor Industry Planning Guide*, Tokyo: Sangyo Times, Inc. (In Japanese.)

Shimizu, S., Kato, Y. *et al.* (2010). Capital Budget, in Kato, Y., Kajiwahara, T. *et al.* (eds.), *The Frontiers of Management Accounting Research*, (pp. 153–172). Tokyo: Chuokeizai-sha. (In Japanese.)

Sugiyama, Y. (2002). *Capital Budget to Improve Investment Efficiency*. Tokyo: Chuokeizai-sha. (In Japanese.)

Sugiyama, Y. (2008). Evaluation of strategic investment: Emergence of a new approach and its examination, *Konan Accounting Research*, Vol. 2, pp. 147–154. Hyogo: Konan University (In Japanese.)

The semiconductor business in the United States is going to overturn. (1984, May 22). *The Nikkei Business Daily*, p. 5. Tokyo: Nikkei Inc.

Yamamoto, M. (1998). *Business Administration in Strategic Investment Decision.* Tokyo: Bunshindo Publishing Corporation (In Japanese.)

Yamamoto, M. (2008). *What Is Accounting?* Tokyo: Kodansha Ltd. (In Japanese.)

Index

Printed in the United States
by Baker & Taylor Publisher Services